ADVANCE PRAISE FOR *CODY'S WISH*

"The rare book that makes you want to cry and cheer at the same time. Horse racing is full of longshots and impossible odds. *Cody's Wish* tells a story that has the heart of a Thoroughbred champion and the soul that beats with the wings of angels. And it's all true. This is so very special."
—**Al Roker**, feature and weather anchor, *Today*; cohost of third hour of *Today*

"'There's no quit in this horse and there's no quit in that young man over there'—so reports Paul K. Halloran Jr. on the true story of a disabled boy and the racehorse he inspired in *Cody's Wish*. Halloran's comprehensive reporting takes readers behind the inspiring story into the lives of the brave boy and the talented Thoroughbred whose love for one another touched a nation." —**Sarah Maslin Nir**, author of *Horse Crazy: The Story of a Woman and a World in Love with an Animal* and two-time finalist for the Pulitzer Prize

"The story of Cody Dorman and Cody's Wish is one of the most unique and meaningful in Breeders' Cup history. It was never just about a great horse winning great races but about the remarkable bond between a boy and a Thoroughbred whose purpose was bigger than the track. Paul Halloran has captured Cody's legacy while chronicling the courage and resilience of the Dorman family. This book ensures that Cody's light, his family's love, and the bond that carried them all into racing's history will never be forgotten. We are honored to see it shared with the world."
—**Drew Fleming**, CEO, Breeders' Cup Limited

"Paul Halloran's poignant book detailing Cody Dorman's valiant fight for life brings full circle the story of Cody and his extraordinary friendship with this special horse. Cody and his family—Kylie, Leslie, and Kelly—embody the true meaning of 'never give up.' Halloran's writing transcends mere moments, masterfully merging the Godolphin stallion's fierce grit during his races with the kitten-like softness he displayed in Cody's presence. Halloran transports us into the deeper realm of the horse and human spirit, a bond beyond measure." —**Jocelyn Russell**, sculptor, Secretariat and Cody's Wish monuments

"A profound story of a remarkable bond between a young man born with Wolf-Hirschhorn syndrome and a courage-driven racehorse. *The Saratoga Special* veteran journalist Paul Halloran takes us on this emotional ride of life and loss, second chances, and the oh-so-powerful impact of love. Written with grace and compassion, Halloran opens the door on persons with disabilities, giving us a unique understanding, a view of hope, and the true belief that when the connection is real, hearts share the same beat."
—**Kim Wickens**, author of *Lexington: The Extraordinary Life and Turbulent Times of America's Legendary Racehorse*

"Who could guess that giving Paul Halloran that Travers Day assignment would provide the perfect opportunity for just the right person to tell the story of Cody Dorman and his family and the great Cody's Wish? Paul's understanding, empathy, and enthusiasm for those involved come out masterfully in his writing, and this book is a must-read for anyone interested in racing. Even those without that passion for racing will be enthralled by this story of courage, compassion, and the unmistakable bond between a boy and a horse." —**Tom Law**, managing editor, *The Saratoga Special*

Cody's Wish

A Boy, a Racehorse, and a Fight for Life

PAUL K. HALLORAN JR.
Foreword by Tom Hammond, NBC Sports

Essex, Connecticut

An imprint of The Globe Pequot Publishing Group, Inc.
64 South Main Street
Essex, CT 06426
www.globepequot.com

Copyright © 2026 by Paul K. Halloran Jr.
Foreword copyright © 2026 by Tom Hammond

All rights reserved. No part of this book may be reproduced in any form or by any electronic or mechanical means, including information storage and retrieval systems, without written permission from the publisher, except by a reviewer who may quote passages in a review.

British Library Cataloguing in Publication Information Available

Library of Congress Cataloging-in-Publication Data available
ISBN 9781493095353 (paperback)
ISBN 9781493095360 (electronic)

Contents

Foreword		vii
Preface		xi
1	Fish Wish	1
2	A Touch on the Shoulder	13
3	"We're Not Doing That"	21
4	Open Heart, Take Two	29
5	Call for a Pizza?	37
6	Life with Cody	49
7	Lifesaver	63
8	New York Traffic	73
9	Junior Achievement	81
10	Winning Formula	87
11	Saratoga Shocker	93
12	Keeneland Reunion	105
13	"That One's for You, Cody"	117
14	Unfinished Business	129
15	California Dreamin'	145

vi Cody's Wish

16	Hold All Tickets	*157*
17	Going Home	*169*
18	Celebration of Lives	*179*

Epilogue 183

Acknowledgments 191

Foreword

ACROSS THIRTY-FOUR YEARS OF BROADCASTING FOR NBC SPORTS, I HAD THE privilege of covering the Olympic Games, the Kentucky Derby, the NFL, the NBA, and Notre Dame football. In a career that spanned fifty total years of sports telecasting, I reported thousands of stories, many both emotional and inspirational.

Given that, there is an irony that the most emotionally powerful story I ever had the chance to tell came after I had officially retired.

In October 2022, NBC Sports was preparing for its annual telecast of the Breeders' Cup World Thoroughbred Championships to be held at Keeneland Race Course in Lexington, Kentucky. After my three-decades-plus stint with NBC Sports, I still knew many of the staffers there. One of them was Jack Felling, now a senior vice president at NBC Sports.

Felling is the best sports feature producer in the business and someone I had worked with many times in the past. Since I live in Lexington and all the NBC folks were in town, it was not a total surprise to get a call from Jack. However, what he said to me was unexpected.

Jack told me they had a Breeders' Cup feature about a teenage boy with a rare medical condition who had bonded with a horse who would be competing in the Breeders' Cup Dirt Mile. Using a bit of flattery as persuasion, Jack told me they had decided that the only narrator who could do the story justice was me.

How could I decline after that? It sounded like a worthy story, and I knew if Jack was involved, it would be well done. So I said, "Yes, please send me the script."

I got the script via email, printed it out, and then sat down on my couch to read it. I was not prepared for the emotional impact of what I was reading. The story of the teen, Cody Dorman; his namesake, the horse

Cody's Wish; and the Dorman family, who provided so much support for Cody as he lived with the genetic disorder known as Wolf-Hirschhorn syndrome, read like a movie script.

I had some familiarity with the horse. Late in August 2022, I had watched Cody's Wish outduel the great champion, Jackie's Warrior, to win the Forego Stakes at Saratoga. But I had no inkling of the poignant story behind the horse's name.

The script laid that all out for me. Thanks to the Make-A-Wish Foundation, Cody, who was wheelchair-bound and forced to use a tablet to communicate, was invited to go to Gainsborough Farm, near Versailles, Kentucky, part of the worldwide Godolphin/Darley racing and breeding operation of Sheikh Mohammed bin Rashid Al Maktoum, the ruler of Dubai. There, Cody was introduced to an unnamed weanling colt sired by the 2007 Breeders' Cup Classic champion, Curlin.

With Cody in his wheelchair, the colt walked over and dropped his head in the boy's lap. That encounter ultimately gave the horse his name. As I read about the bond that, against all expectations, seemed to persist between a boy who had drawn such a tough lot in life and a Thoroughbred racehorse who had grown to be a champion, I felt tears running down my cheeks.

The NBC Sports crew came to my house to record my narration. By the time of Breeders' Cup day, I had been emailed a finished copy of the feature. In the Keeneland Club that day, I was seated with friends and acquaintances from the University of Kentucky's Martin-Gatton College of Agriculture, Food and Environment. On my phone, I showed them the story of Cody's Wish and Cody Dorman. By the time it had finished, everyone who had watched had tears in their eyes.

I don't know if I've ever wanted a horse to win a race any more than I wanted Cody's Wish to win the 2022 Dirt Mile. Even though I knew Cody's Wish liked to come from off the pace, my heart sank when the horse was in last place in the turn for home. But, as if propelled by a larger force, Cody's Wish started moving forward. He was third at the quarter pole, second at the top of the stretch, and then, after a scintillating stretch battle with Cyberknife, he was a Breeders' Cup champion by a head.

By then, my friends from the University of Kentucky who had cried at seeing the feature on my phone were cheering wildly. When the NBC Sports telecast cut to people stopping by sixteen-year-old Cody Dorman's wheelchair to congratulate him, they started crying again. Cry, cheer, cry—Cody's Wish made it that kind of Breeders' Cup day.

Foreword

Tales of the bond between man and horse have been the stuff of legend for millennia. As someone who has loved horses since I was a little boy, there was something exhilarating in seeing what Cody's Wish meant in the life of Cody Dorman. "He saved my life," Cody once said of the horse.

This notion may be fanciful, but it seemed that Cody's Wish also benefited from the relationship. Famously, the horse was winless in his first three starts. That is, until Cody Dorman and his family showed up to see him run. From that point forward, usually with Cody Dorman there by the racetrack, Cody's Wish won eleven of thirteen races, including finishing his career with a repeat victory in the 2023 Breeders' Cup Dirt Mile.

Beyond the connection between boy and horse, this is also the story of Cody Dorman's loving family, parents Kelly and Leslie and younger sister Kylie. Author Paul Halloran is the father of a special-needs daughter and brings a unique understanding of the daunting physical and emotional challenges the Dormans faced in raising Cody, a child the doctors said would not reach two years old but who lived to be seventeen. You will see that Cody's family members are heroes in this story.

Three years after I narrated the story of Cody Dorman and Cody's Wish for NBC Sports, I still have people tell me how much it impacted them. I can assure you, this book will make you weep, cheer, smile, and weep again. It contains a story you will not soon forget.

Tom Hammond, NBC Sports

Preface

An email from *The Saratoga Special* managing editor Tom Law arrived at 9:34 a.m. August 27, 2022, with the Travers Day writing assignments. One of my races to cover was the Forego Stakes, which seemed like a break on what would be an arduous day, with six stakes races to be covered by the *Special* team. Jackie's Warrior was the heaviest of favorites and I had plenty of background, having written about him when he won a Saratoga stakes as a two-year-old in 2020 and having watched him win two more stakes in 2021. It looked like the story could almost be written before the race and then filled in with quotes and some details.

The best-laid plans . . .

Jackie's Warrior went to the lead, as expected, in the Forego, but he was overtaken late in the stretch by a fast-closing Cody's Wish, an 8–1 longshot. After the race, Sean Clancy, co-owner of the *Special* with his brother, Joe, told me, "There's a story behind that horse. You should look into it."

With our next edition not coming out for four days, there was time for a deep dive. Michael Banahan, director of bloodstock for the United States division of Godolphin, a worldwide Thoroughbred racing and breeding operation, connected me with Mary Bourne at Gainsborough Farm in Versailles, Kentucky, where Cody's Wish—and, as it turned out, this too-good-to-be-true-but-it-is story—was born.

That led to a phone interview with Kelly Dorman, who told me about his son, Cody, for whom Cody's Wish was named. Kelly was generous with his time and information, sharing personal details with a writer he had never met. He said Cody was born with Wolf-Hirschhorn syndrome, a rare genetic disease that causes congenital heart defects, intellectual disability, and other serious problems. Cody spent the first twelve days of his life in the neonatal intensive care unit and had two heart surgeries by the time he was five weeks old. One doctor told Kelly and his wife, Leslie, that Cody wouldn't make it to his second birthday.

The longer he talked, the more compelling the story became. In reporter parlance, it was pure gold, and especially impactful for a parent of a young adult with profound autism. I asked Kelly whether Cody would be willing to answer a few questions, and an interview was set up.

Asked about his connection to Cody's Wish, Cody said, through the tablet he used to communicate, "He's my buddy. I love him. He gives me so much motivation."

I sent Kelly a video of my daughter, Martha, introducing herself to Cody and another of her riding a horse.

"That made Cody smile," Kelly wrote. "That's so cool."

Cody sent Martha a joke: "What day do fish hate? Fryday."

Priceless.

The story on the Forego covered a lot of ground and came out to 1,783 words. Joe Clancy was, as usual, on target with his headline: "Fairytale: Cody's Wish Delivers Emotional Upset for Namesake in Gr. 1."

It was nice to have the story earn an honorable mention in the News/Enterprise category of the media Eclipse Awards, a writing competition run in conjunction with horse racing's annual end-of-year honors presented to the champions in each division.

A few months later, after Cody's Wish won the Breeders' Cup Dirt Mile, Cody was announced as the recipient of the Big Sport of Turfdom Award, given to someone who enhances media coverage of Thoroughbred racing. Knowing I had taken an interest in the story, Tom asked whether I wanted to write a column around the time of the award presentation in Arizona.

After revisiting the story and conducting another lengthy phone interview with Kelly, I started to think about a book. I called Kelly on January 2, 2023, and ran it by him. I said the idea would be to tell the story of Cody as well as the champion horse named for him. I was up front and said that in almost forty years of writing, I had done thousands of newspaper and magazine stories but never anything longer than a multipart series. A book was definitely on my to-do list, but I had given it serious thought only a few times.

It's always easier to find reasons not to do something than to do it, but this was different. This had three of my worlds colliding: horse racing, writing, and special needs. There was an obvious connection with Kelly right from the start, so this project had a now-or-never feel to it.

Kelly loved the idea but, like any smart husband, said he would run it by his "CEO," wife Leslie. The three of us met by Zoom the next day, and I gave Leslie the same pitch. I told them it would require a leap of faith to entrust their story to a first-time author but reinforced my confidence in being able to do it justice and my passion to get it right. Leslie approved, and it was time to get to work.

After deciding that Sunday night was a good time for all of us, we did the first Zoom interview January 8, 2023. Over the next several months, through weekly electronic meetings, Kelly and Leslie gave me the backstory. Invariably, I would get off the Zoom and share with my wife, Julie, another amazing anecdote.

My first trip to Kentucky to meet the Dormans in person came in April 2023, scheduled to coincide with the spring meet at Keeneland, a gem of a racetrack I had somehow never visited. It turned out to be an extremely productive—and profitable—five days. I managed to do more than a half dozen interviews for the book, visit two of my favorite horses (stallions Curlin and Catholic Boy), and win Keeneland's spring handicapping tournament, the Grade 1 Gamble.

Most important, I spent a lot of time with Kelly, Leslie, Cody, and Cody's sister, Kylie (my favorite).

And I followed Cody's Wish around the country in 2023. Churchill Downs on Kentucky Derby Day. Belmont Park for the Met Mile. The Whitney at Saratoga, when my friends and I were honored to have Cody as the guest of honor at our annual Whitney Eve barbecue. Santa Anita for the Breeders' Cup, the last race for Cody's Wish, with his best friend there to cheer him on.

It didn't take long for the relationship with the Dormans to go from professional to deeply personal. They are family now—whether they like it or not. As you get to know them in the pages ahead, I think you'll agree God knew exactly what He was doing when He sent Cody to them.

After a few months of talking with Kelly and Leslie, I told them I had a singular goal for this book: that they feel I did a good job telling their son's story.

I hope you do, too.

The story of Cody Dorman and Cody's Wish first appeared in *The Saratoga Special* in 2022. DORMAN FAMILY.

1

Fish Wish

By the time he was approaching his thirteenth birthday, Cody Dorman had already beaten the odds.

Born with a rare and debilitating genetic disease, he was supposed to be dead before he turned two, according to what one doctor told his parents. Yet, even when Cody was referred to Make-A-Wish Foundation in 2018, it was not necessarily an indication death was imminent.

"We are not a last-wish organization," said Faith Hacker, former director of corporate engagement for Make-A-Wish in central Kentucky, noting that 80 percent of the kids who receive a wish go on to live fulfilling lives. "We have some studies where doctors have said we truly provide hope. Kids have a renewed sense of energy and parents talk about how it improves their mental health."

Hacker could very well have been talking about the parents, too.

"You get to be normal for a while," Kelly Dorman said.

"Normal" was not a word typically associated with Cody's existence. By the summer of 2018, the twelve-year-old had already undergone more than forty operations—two of them open-heart surgeries before he turned four—and had been living on a feeding tube since he was six months old.

Cody had been acting like he was in distress, screaming and generally feeling miserable, but X-rays and other tests couldn't pinpoint the issue. He was deemed a candidate for palliative care, the goal being to try to relieve his pain and make him comfortable, while maintaining the highest quality of life.

On the cusp of becoming a teenager, Cody used his communication tablet to tell his parents, Kelly and Leslie, that for his Make-A-Wish trip he wanted to go to Bass Pro Shops headquarters and the Wonders of Wildlife National Museum and Aquarium in Springfield, Missouri. That was a less traditional request than Disney World or meeting a famous athlete, but understandable since he had grown up with a competitive angler for a father, whose passion for fishing had been passed on to his son.

Cody's choice brought back memories for Kelly and Leslie, who had taken him to a Bass Pro Shops in Clarksville, Indiana, when he was six months old, May 27, 2006—the first time they took him out of the house for any reason other than a medical appointment.

"It was one of the first times we ever saw him smile," Leslie said.

The week before the trip, Make-A-Wish threw a party for Cody, his family, and friends on a houseboat on Laurel River Lake in Corbin, Kentucky, roughly an hour south of Richmond, Kentucky, where the Dormans live. Two dozen people gathered to celebrate Cody and wish him well, including four close friends who would travel to Missouri with the Dormans: John and Tammy Myers; their son, Brad; and his wife, Nae.

Cody's original wish was to visit Bass Pro Shops headquarters.
DORMAN FAMILY.

They own Backwater Outfitters, where Kelly had been buying bait and other fishing equipment for fifteen years, even before the Myers family took it over. Kelly often brought Cody to the store and the boy developed a close friendship with the Myerses, so when it came time for his Make-A-Wish trip to Bass Pro Shops, he asked whether they could come along.

"I want Backwaters to go," Cody told his parents.

"Backwaters obviously meant me and Dad and our family," Brad Myers said. "That was super exciting for all of us. Listen, the first time that little fella said, 'I love you' on that tablet, I'm six five, three hundred pounds, and I cried like a baby. You talk to him just like you do any kid, and then twelve years later, he's able to talk back to you for the first time. That was something."

Cody had a specific request as part of his wish: He wanted his friend Mark Zona to take him through the wildlife museum. Introduced to Cody six years earlier at Backwaters, Zona grew up in the Chicago suburbs, discovered bass fishing as a kid, and was immediately hooked. He entered his first bass tournament when he was nine and knew early on what he wanted to do when he grew up.

Zona got a call in 2004 from someone identifying himself as an ESPN producer wanting to talk about hosting a show, and, thinking it was a prank, he hung up. Fortunately, the producer called back and Zona ended up cohosting *Loudmouth Bass*, the start of a TV career that has stretched more than twenty years.

When Zona met Cody at Backwaters, it didn't take him long to be struck by the boy's courage in the face of unimaginable adversity.

"I'm crying my ass off, just talking about him. That's what Cody has meant to me," Zona said. "That young man has been an inspiration. He is a frickin' warrior."

Cody once had a dream that involved a yellow Labrador retriever saving his life. He asked his parents for a dog, but yellow Labs are prolific shedders, not meant for a child with respiratory issues. Leslie and Cody came across a miniature schnauzer who gravitated to Cody, so he asked for a dog like that instead. This breed is hypoallergenic and does not shed, so the Dormans added a family member, and Cody named him after his second-favorite fisherman: Zona.

The Dormans made the nine-hour drive to Big Cedar Lodge on Table Rock Lake, on the Missouri-Arkansas border, in September 2018, their first away-from-home vacation since Cody was born. It's one of those places where you can hold up your phone, point it in any direction, and take a postcard-worthy photo.

On his Make-A-Wish trip, Cody met his fisherman friend Mark Zona. DORMAN FAMILY.

Zona had a full slate that weekend, between the Bass Fishing Hall of Fame induction and filming commercials for Bass Pro Shops, but he carved out a two-hour window to spend with Cody. When time ran out and he got a call requesting his presence elsewhere, he sent word that he would be there when he got there. He wasn't about to cut short his visit with someone he considered a friend, let alone a Make-A-Wish child.

"I wanted it to be an unbelievable experience for that young man and his family," said Zona, who wasn't the only big name Cody encountered on his trip. Zona set him up to meet Kevin Van Dam, the Michael Jordan of bass fishing—or was Jordan the Kevin Van Dam of basketball?—and Dave Mercer, a media personality in the angling world.

Kelly, who enjoyed the trip at least as much as his son, brought some "Casting for Cody" T-shirts that had been made for a fundraising event back home. Mercer and Van Dam wore them onstage at the Bassmaster

Classic the next year, elevating Cody to rock-star status on the fishing circuit long before he became a household name in Thoroughbred racing.

Cody loved everything about the trip, especially the golf-cart ride through Lost Canyon Cave, a two-and-a-half-mile journey through rock formations, handcrafted bridges, and tumbling waterfalls. Every day at Big Cedar Lodge ends with the Top of the Rock Sunset Ceremony, outside a stone church overlooking Table Rock Lake. As the sun sets behind the Ozarks, men dressed as Civil War soldiers play the bagpipes and a cannon is fired.

"It's one of the most picturesque things I've ever seen," Zona said of the ceremony, which has been attended by the likes of President George W. Bush and actor Kevin Costner. "What [Bass Pro Shops founder] Johnny Morris has created up there is visually stunning."

Unbeknownst to the Dormans, the ceremony that night was dedicated to Cody. They were brought to a de facto VIP area for the cannon blast, and one of the soldiers gave Cody his cap and the wad of paper loaded into the cannon before firing. He told Cody he had been wearing the same hat for twenty years, but he wanted him to have it.

"I don't think there was a dry eye there that night," Kelly said.

Actually, there might have been two, according to Brad Myers.

"When that cannon went off, Cody giggled," he said. "It was pretty awesome."

A month after that trip of a lifetime, Cody was asked to be an ambassador on Make-A-Wish Day at Keeneland Race Course, a major fundraiser for the organization that strives to create life-changing experiences for children with critical illnesses. Horseman John Greeley came up with the idea in 2007 to expose the racing community to Make-A-Wish and vice versa.

On Make-A-Wish Day, children get matched with participating horse farms that serve as sponsors but do much more than write a check. Prior to spending an afternoon at the Keeneland racetrack, each kid visits a farm and gets a behind-the-scenes look at Thoroughbred racing in its purest form—a view the industry would benefit from more people experiencing.

Cody was paired with Godolphin, a racing operation owned by Sheikh Mohammed bin Rashid Al Maktoum, ruler of Dubai. Cody was invited to visit Gainsborough Farm in Versailles, around twelve miles from Keeneland.

Cody came to Gainsborough on October 11, 2018, with his parents and younger sister, Kylie. He was sitting in the chair in which he spent virtually all of his waking hours, which presented a concern for the Godolphin staff. Nobody knows how horses will react to changes in their environment, especially young foals in the presence of a boy in a souped-up wheelchair.

Danny Mulvihill, the farm manager, kept that in mind while considering which horses to bring out to meet Cody. He had no idea how significant that decision would be.

According to the Jockey Club, there were 19,770 Thoroughbreds born in the United States in 2018, including forty at Gainsborough Farm. By May 3, most of the Godolphin foals had arrived, but Dance Card, a $750,000 purchase as a two-year-old in 2011, had yet to deliver.

Godolphin had paid a premium for the filly's bloodlines and her potential as a broodmare. Dance Card is a daughter of Tapit, considered one of the best stallions in North America. By the end of 2023, he had topped the sire list three times and was the all-time leading North American sire by progeny earnings. A grandson of Hall of Famer A.P. Indy, Tapit carries a pedigree including Triple Crown winners Seattle Slew and the immortal Secretariat.

On the dam side, Dance Card is a granddaughter of Belmont Stakes winner Editor's Note, with bloodlines that include two-year-old champions Forty Niner and Devil's Bag, as well as influential stallion Mr. Prospector. The $750,000 price tag was the second highest at Fasig-Tipton's February select two-year-old sale in Florida. (Godolphin also had the most expensive purchase, spending $1.35 million for a filly named Betwixt, who never made it to the races and had a nondescript career as a broodmare.)

During her career, Dance Card won four races, topped by the Grade 1 Gazelle Stakes in 2012, and earned $502,200. Godolphin bred her to its stallion Medaglia d'Oro in 2014 and 2015 and then sent her to Ghostzapper in 2016. In 2017, she had a date with the mighty Curlin, a two-time Horse of the Year and prolific sire with a $150,000 stud fee that would rise to $250,000 by 2024.

The mating took place at Hill 'n' Dale Farm May 19, 2017, a warm day in Lexington when the temperature reached eighty-two degrees. Dance Card returned to Gainsborough in foal—pregnant—and fifty weeks later she was ready to give birth.

Mares typically drop their foals late at night, sometimes in the wee hours, and Mulvihill makes a point to be there for all of them. Dance Card produced her Curlin foal at 11:16 p.m. on May 3, 2018, in what was an uneventful birth.

"It wasn't anything special," Mulvihill recalled. "The ones that stand out when you're foaling are the ones you have problems with. Everything about this one was very normal."

Mulvihill had nieces visiting from Virginia, and he invited them to watch the foaling. They ended up recording it, not realizing how significant the video would be until three years later.

Dance Card and her foal, who would eventually be named Cody's Wish, enjoy some paddock time. GODOLPHIN.

When Cody and his family arrived on Make-A-Wish Day, they were greeted by Mulvihill and Mary Bourne, the office manager at Gainsborough. Mulvihill took them on a tour of the expansive property, which includes a forty-eight-bedroom house used only when Sheikh Mohammed is in town. The last stop was Barn One, where Mulvihill planned to show Cody some mares and foals, hoping he could have a meaningful interaction with one of the babies.

Mulvihill pulled out two mares with their foals for Cody but did not attempt to get close with them. The best chance for an up-close-and-personal meeting, he had determined, would be the Dance Card foal.

"The reason we picked him was because he was so laid back and we figured that was the best chance to get him up close to Cody in the wheelchair," Mulvihill said. "He was one of our nicer, more straightforward foals."

Cody, wearing tan pants, a red plaid shirt, and a black jacket, looked on as Mulvihill approached with Dance Card and the bay (reddish-brown) foal. In addition to being bigger than the typical five-month-old Thoroughbred, the horse was easily identifiable by a splotch of white on his forehead—a diamond-like mark symmetrical enough to catch a jeweler's attention.

Mulvihill brought the foal forward to stand in front of Cody. They looked at each other, the boy trying to figure out what to make of the horse and the horse sizing up the boy in the wheelchair. The moment was already working out better than anyone expected, when, unexpectedly, the foal gently laid his head on Cody's lap.

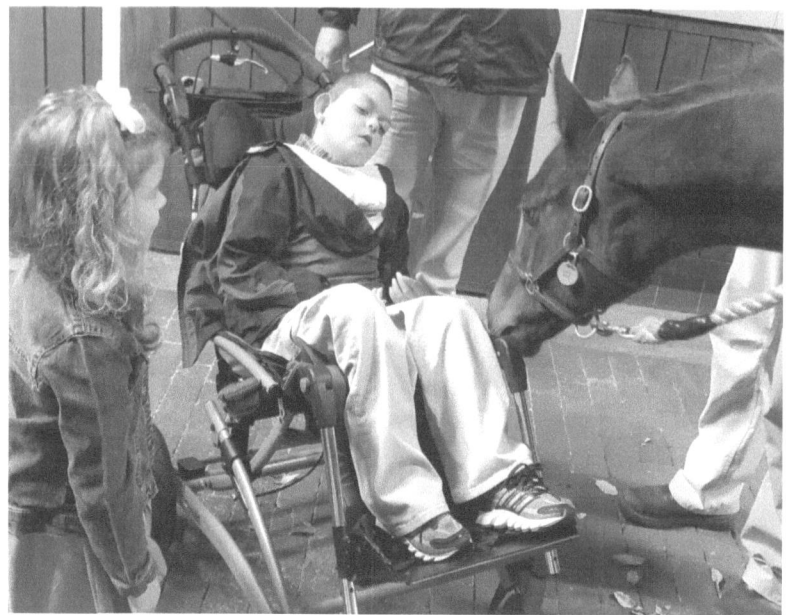

The first meeting of Cody and Cody's Wish took place at Gainsborough Farm on October 11, 2018. DORMAN FAMILY.

Cody smiled, his way of expressing approval. Those who witnessed the interaction were taken aback by the instant connection, especially considering the dynamics.

"That was the first wheelchair kid we've had," Mulvihill said. "That's a huge concern. I am fairly cautious, for the horse's safety and for the safety of everybody around them. Unless I'm comfortable, I don't try to push it, but it was apparent right away how comfortable the foal felt. When he came out, he stopped to check things out. Sometimes these foals don't like children. I've seen it with my own kids around the foals. They look at these little humans and they say, 'Whoa, what's that?' But he didn't. He was all about it. He stopped and looked, and we just encouraged him forward a little bit, and he came right up and just kept coming to Cody. It made everybody take a step back and just watch. It was awesome."

When Mulvihill got back to the office, he relayed the story to Mary Bourne, who was preparing to accompany the Dormans to Keeneland for Make-A-Wish Day. The encounter made a lasting impression on Mulvihill, and just hearing about it had the same effect on Bourne.

Keeneland rolls out the red carpet for the Make-A-Wish kids and their families, hosting them in the Phoenix Room overlooking the paddock and dedicating a race to them. Kelly is far from a big gambler, but he wasn't about to spend a day at Keeneland without going to the windows. On this day, he couldn't do anything wrong.

"I think I won money on every race except the one they dedicated to Cody," he said. "I don't bet a whole lot, but it was pretty neat."

One horse who caught his eye was Irish Oak, a two-year-old in a maiden race (for horses who have not yet won in their careers). Kelly figured he had just spent the morning with a salt-of-the-earth guy from Ireland in Mulvihill, so why not bet that one? Irish Oak won and paid $35.80 for a $2 win bet, or, in Kelly's case, $358 for $20. The luck of the Irish indeed.

The Dormans had their picture taken in the winner's circle after the race honoring Cody and, between Godolphin and Keeneland, went home with a bag full of mementos. But the intangibles far outweighed the trinkets. Not only was it a chance to experience horse racing as VIPs, but it also provided a respite from the psychological burden of caring for a son with unspeakably severe disabilities.

"It takes you away from the medical stuff for just a little bit," Leslie said.

Any time not thinking about medical problems was time well spent for the Dormans—something that came back into focus a month later when a blood vessel in Cody's stomach burst and he ended up in the hospital. "That was very painful for him and he really suffered," Kelly said.

Spending time with the Make-A-Wish families at Gainsborough is also therapeutic for Bourne, who is constantly impressed by the resilience of people like the Dormans.

"Make-A-Wish has always been one of our big charities," she said. "We get so much out of it. It really is a special day. You see the happiness it brings to all the kids and their families and you feel so blessed when you leave. It really is a humbling day."

That's what Make-A-Wish is about—providing experiences to help kids who have been dealt a horrible hand forget about their problems, even if only for a short period.

The Dormans stayed in touch with both Mulvihill and Bourne, a Godolphin employee since 1985, when she started working in Sheikh Mohammed's mansion at Gainsborough. Her official title is office manager, but she is considered the glue in a finely tuned operation. In 2018, she and Mulvihill were among one hundred Godolphin veteran employees worldwide invited to dinner at Sheikh Mohammed's palace in Dubai.

Mulvihill came to the United States in 1996 from Kildare, an Irish horse racing hub an hour southwest of Dublin. He found a job at Knockgriffin

Farm in Paris, Kentucky, just up the road from Lexington, owned by fellow Irishman Jim Fitzgerald.

Mulvihill was in McCarthy's Irish Bar in downtown Lexington one night when he met Carol Illston, an expatriate from England who also worked on a horse farm. They began dating, managed to overcome the English/Irish hurdle—not insignificant—and decided to move to Ireland together in 1998, with a six-month stop in England to help Carol's dad sell his ostrich farm.

Mulvihill got a job with Darley, the Godolphin US breeding operation, and stayed for ten years before he and Carol left for Japan, where he managed a stallion farm. They got married in 2000 and moved back to Kentucky in 2013, settling in a house on the grounds of Gainsborough with their five children.

Neither Mulvihill nor Bourne could have ever anticipated how much the initial interaction between Cody and the Dance Card foal would impact them going forward.

Around a year after that first meeting, Kelly was shopping for bait at Backwater Outfitters when he got a call from Bourne.

"Do you remember the day you were here and that little foal came up and put his head on Cody's lap?" she asked him.

She must have been kidding.

"I remember it like it was five minutes ago," Kelly told her. "That was pretty neat."

"I hope you don't mind, but we just named that horse after Cody: Cody's Wish," Bourne said.

Kelly instantly got chills, the kind you get when someone throws a bucket of ice water on you.

"I didn't know what to say," he said, which might come as a surprise to those close to him who have jokingly tabbed him "Chatty Cathy," after the Mattel talking doll from the early 1960s.

Naming the horse for Cody was a deviation from past practice for Godolphin.

"We make a point not to do it because it becomes very difficult to draw a line," Godolphin USA chief operating officer Dan Pride said. "We don't name them after employees. We try to keep it so we don't get in a situation where we approve one for somebody and then somebody else wants to name [a horse] for their grandchild. So it is very unusual that we did it. Mary Bourne gets credit for that."

The official registration of Thoroughbred names falls under the auspices of the Jockey Club, which enforces various rules about naming racehorses.

At the urging of Mary Bourne (shown with Kylie Dorman at the 2022 Breeders' Cup), Godolphin went against its own protocol in naming Cody's Wish. DORMAN FAMILY.

For a name to be reused, the previous horse must be beyond age ten and unraced for at least five years. There were two racehorses named Cody's Wish in the quarter century prior: a Quarter Horse born in 1993 who never raced, and a Thoroughbred foaled in 2003 who won three of seventeen races at Great Lakes Downs in Michigan. That made Cody's Wish available and Godolphin reserved it, planning to use it for the Dance Card foal Cody had met when it came time to officially register the colt for his racing career.

Once Kelly gathered himself, he repeated to Bourne something he had said to Mulvihill a year earlier.

"If that horse has half the heart that Cody's got, he's going to be pretty awesome."

 2

A Touch on the Shoulder

LESLIE DORMAN WAS IN A STATE OF MEDICATED EUPHORIA, BARELY ALERT enough to know something was not right.

She had just given birth to a baby boy she and her husband Kelly named Cody. The first indication that something was amiss was when the nurses took Cody away rather than laying him on her chest.

"Why are they taking my baby away?" she thought to herself, but being a first-time mother unsure of all the childbirth protocols and still in a fog from the drugs, she didn't immediately speak up.

Leslie thought it odd that Kelly would also leave her side in the labor room at Lexington's Baptist Health Hospital so soon after Cody was born on December 18, 2005. When he returned, his look and demeanor jolted his wife. He didn't look or act like an ebullient first-time father.

"I still didn't know what was going on," Leslie said. "I didn't know there was something wrong with Cody, but I knew I didn't get to see him right away. When Kelly came back in the room, I knew he wasn't happy."

Leslie asked how much their son weighed and was told five pounds, eleven ounces—appreciably less than the eight pounds her doctor had projected, but not necessarily a cause for alarm. Kelly left again, this time for a longer period, leaving Leslie accompanied only by her thoughts.

She was not aware Cody had been hustled to the neonatal intensive care unit, requiring oxygen to help him take his first breaths. Kelly was beckoned to an office, where Dr. John Walker delivered some sobering news.

"I was completely oblivious to the birthing process and everything else," Kelly said. "We went to all the classes and read all the books and everything you could think of, but I just wasn't prepared. Dr. Walker took me in his office, and I remember getting mad when he told me a lot of stuff I didn't want to hear."

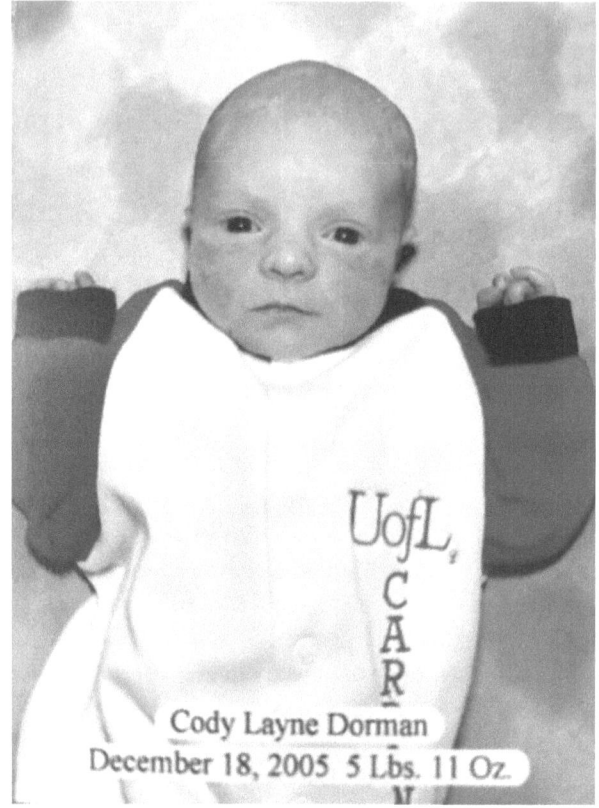

Cody was born on December 18, 2005. DORMAN FAMILY.

Prior to that moment, Kelly's biggest problem that week was Leslie going into labor during the University of Louisville–University of Kentucky men's basketball game on December 17. Less than twenty-four hours later, the 73–61 loss incurred by Kelly's beloved Cardinals suddenly was not such a big deal, even in a state where seemingly everyone wears red or blue, harboring undying loyalty to their school and varying levels of contempt for the other.

Now Kelly (a former all-star football player), Leslie, and their baby boy would be facing an opponent they had never heard of. And Dr. Walker told him they were big underdogs.

A heart murmur was of immediate concern and would require surgery, sooner rather than later. Cody had a valve in his heart that was not opening fully, restricting blood flow. But the newborn's heart and need for oxygen support were not the only red flags.

"He just ran down a list of potential problems Cody would have," Kelly said.

The new father heard the doctor's words, understood some, and hated all of them.

"I remember feeling a lot of resentment toward him. It was almost like I was going numb," Kelly said. "I was receptive to what he was saying, but I don't know if I was accepting it, if that makes any sense. I don't think anybody can accept hearing things like that, especially with your first baby."

Kelly barely had time to process the news when Dr. Walker gave him a task he wanted no part of.

"When he first told me, I kind of took it as him being kind of cold-hearted and just running the numbers," Kelly said. "But he wasn't that way. We didn't know anything about anything, medically. He told me to go back and explain it to Leslie."

Not so fast, Doc.

"I asked if he would go with me," Kelly said. "As much as I wasn't liking him at that moment, I knew I needed him."

The doctor agreed to be the co-bearer of bad news and accompanied Kelly to Leslie's room. At this point, there were several family members there, hoping to meet the newborn, who had begun the fight for his life in the NICU. Kelly asked them to leave so he and Dr. Walker could speak with Leslie.

"I wanted her to hear it without an audience," Kelly said, "even though they were family."

Now Leslie was sure something was seriously wrong.

Once the room had been cleared, Dr. Walker repeated for Leslie what he had told Kelly about the myriad challenges Cody would be facing—in the short term and, if he survived, the long.

Leslie, now fully awake, was hysterical.

"I will never forget her screaming and crying. I can still hear it now, the pain in her heart from hearing this," said Kelly. "It was so hard for her to hear those words."

There was not yet an official diagnosis—Cody was only hours old—but there was a preliminary prognosis, and it wasn't positive.

"It was just so many unknowns," Kelly said. "The doctor kind of laid out what we might have ahead of us. His heart murmur was extremely bad. I think he knew just from that alone the path we'd have to take to fix that."

The news was bad, but neither Kelly nor Leslie was willing to ask the obvious question: Is our baby going to die?

"They didn't really say at the time whether he would make it or not, but I know they were thinking about that," Kelly said.

In addition to the heart issue, which presented almost immediately after Cody was born, there would be serious developmental issues, among other major problems.

As the shock started to subside, the parents were told they could visit their baby in the NICU. No one wants to see a newborn hooked up to oxygen, but to his parents Cody looked like a fighter, even as a sub-six-pound infant in a critical care unit.

Cody survived those first hours and days, celebrating his first Christmas at Baptist Health and providing a sneak preview of the fighter he would become.

Like any new parents, even those with a very sick baby, the Dormans were anxious to take their little boy home. There were several false starts, the nurses telling them Cody would be discharged, only to have a setback keep him hospitalized. On December 29, Kelly and Leslie were told Cody could be discharged the following day, but there was a stipulation: They had to stay in a room with him overnight before they could take him home.

"Don't be staring at him all night," a nurse recommended. "Just go on about your things."

As anyone would, the Dormans did little but look at their son until they heard the door open.

"I knew you all would be standing looking over him," the nurse said.

Cody still required oxygen when his parents got him home to Georgetown, around thirteen miles from Lexington. Leslie and Kelly applied it, marking the beginning of their on-the-job training as de facto home health aides. They quickly realized just how sick he was.

"His heart murmur was so bad, I could actually hear it," Kelly said. "They let us listen to it. You didn't have to be a doctor to know what was going on. They were wanting to let him grow and get a little bit stronger before they tried to do anything."

A month later, Cody still wasn't doing well and doctors had no choice but to operate. Cody had pulmonary valve stenosis—narrowing of a heart valve—and the plan was to open the pulmonary valve using a catheterization procedure. The Dormans were referred to Dr. Carol Cottrill, a cardiac surgeon at the University of Kentucky Medical Center (UKMC), prompting Kelly to hit the pause button on his ingrained animus for all things UK.

The doctor told Kelly and Leslie there was a 98 percent chance Cody would make it through the surgery. "But when you're sitting in that waiting room, that 2 percent looks awful big," Kelly said.

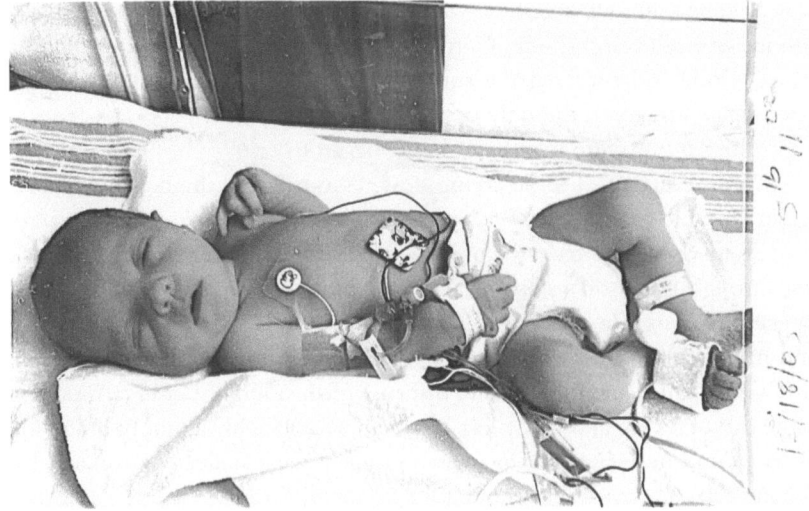
Cody faced serious medical problems from the time he was born. DORMAN FAMILY.

Perhaps it was fitting that they were sent to Cottrill, who could relate better than most to the anguish they were feeling. She was debilitated by severe rheumatoid arthritis, requiring a custom-built support so she could stand for surgeries. Beyond any physical pain she was forced to endure, she carried emotional scars she tried to keep parents such as the Dormans from experiencing.

Living in Lexington in the late 1960s, with no college degree, Cottrill had four children and a household to run. When her youngest child, Crystal, developed heart disease and started treatment at Cincinnati Children's Hospital, Cottrill became interested in the work of the people trying to help her.

She started taking evening classes as her curiosity transitioned to vocation, eventually switching to school during the day so she could take more courses. When Crystal died after Cottrill's second year of classes, she considered dropping out, but the tragedy inspired her to complete her studies.

Cottrill was one of five women—out of 107 total—in the University of Cincinnati Medical School Class of 1971. She didn't intend to take care of babies, but something about those little beings captured her attention. She had been practicing for about four years when she and her husband, Tom, took in the first of their thirty foster children. The director of the pediatric intensive care unit at UKMC, she became active with the Lexington-based nonprofit Children of the Americas, taking annual medical mission trips to Guatemala until her death in 2017 at age eighty.

Several hours after starting what was supposed to have been a relatively routine procedure on Cody, Cottrill emerged from the OR, drenched in sweat. Cody had survived the surgery, but it was not successful, leaving open-heart surgery as the only option to keep him alive.

The parents were jolted and Leslie began to cry.

"You don't need to be crying now," Cottrill told them. "I'll tell you when it's time to cry."

As the Dormans tried to come to grips with the idea of a surgeon sawing through their son's sternum, Cody almost didn't make it back to the operating room. He was in the pediatric ICU at UKMC when he coded and his parents were escorted out. A peripherally inserted central catheter (PICC)—a long, thin tube used to dispense medication or liquid nutrition—came out of his leg and Cody lost a lot of blood, roughly a pint of blood for every pound he weighed. Doctors and nurses got it under control, and by the next day he was stable enough for the open-heart procedure—not that there was much of a choice.

This time Kelly and Leslie were told the odds of survival were closer to 75 percent. That sounds promising, until you try to digest that there's a one in four chance you will have to pick out a coffin for your five-week-old child.

Nonetheless, the odds were in Cody's favor, and, just before he went under the knife, in the minds and hearts of his parents, his chances got inexplicably and immeasurably better.

With only two visitors at a time allowed, Leslie was a constant presence at her son's bedside, while Kelly rotated with grandparents and other family members. At one point when Leslie was alone with Cody, Kelly returned and she asked him what he had wanted a few minutes earlier.

"I didn't know what she was talking about," Kelly said. "From the waiting room, I could look through the glass and see right into Cody's room. I told her there was no one in the room but her and Cody."

That made no sense to Leslie. She might have been oblivious to just about everything other than her helpless infant son, but she hadn't lost feeling in her body. When someone touches us, specialized receptor cells in our skin relay a signal through our nerves to the brain. And Leslie knew what her brain had told her.

"They were getting ready to take him into surgery," Leslie said. "I was just torn up. I was standing there praying over him, and I got this light touch on my shoulder. I didn't look up. I just kept praying."

Kelly assured Leslie there was no one else in the room—at least no one who could be seen. There was no logical explanation, but it did prompt Leslie to recalculate the odds of Cody's surviving to 100 percent.

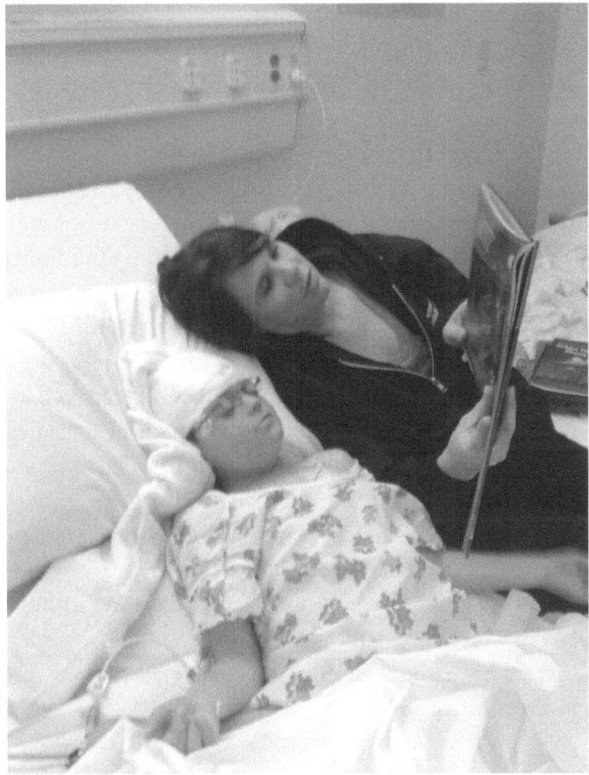

Cody's parents were a constant presence during his many hospital stays. DORMAN FAMILY.

"Kelly, he's going to be OK," she told her husband. "He's going to make it through this surgery and he's going to be fine."

She and her son weren't alone in that hospital room.

"I knew God had His hands wrapped around that child and He had His hands wrapped around us," Leslie said. "He was telling us, 'I got him. Let Me take care of it.'"

Kelly wasn't going to argue, especially when he felt the sense of calm that suddenly enveloped his wife.

"She had a peace about her after that," he said. "There was one Leslie when I left the room and a different Leslie when I came back."

If there is such a thing as a simple open-heart surgery on an incredibly frail five-week-old, this was it. The surgeon used a scalpel to open Cody's pulmonary valve so blood could flow properly.

"The doctor said it was actually one of the easiest heart surgeries he had done in some time," Kelly said. "I think there was a lot of concern before they went in, more so than what they were letting us know. For open-heart surgery, this went as well as anyone could have expected."

Kelly and Leslie were alarmed when they saw their son in the recovery room.

"I will never forget that image, walking in there for the first time after that surgery," Kelly said. "To see that many wires and hoses and other stuff hooked up to him pretty much from head to toe was a pretty big shock.

"They had a drain tube and that tube was nothing but fluid and blood. It just constantly kept dripping into a bag. There was just so much fluid. And I'm like, 'Where in the world is all this coming from? How can somebody that small have that much come out of him?'"

The Dormans didn't realize it, but they had only arrived at base camp on what would become a Mount Everest of medical maladies. Yet they were becoming acutely aware of the limitless fortitude crammed into their tiny son's body—and soul.

"You're sitting there thinking, 'How in the world can he pull through something like this?'" Kelly said. "That kind of trauma, being that small. And I guess that's when Cody really first started teaching us how much grit and fire he has in him. He wasn't going to quit."

Neither were his parents, though the challenges to their resolve, were, like Cody, in their infant stages.

3

"We're Not Doing That"

THE DORMANS BROUGHT THEIR TWELVE-DAY-OLD ILL BUNDLE OF JOY HOME December 30, 2005. They knew he was very sick, but it ended up taking roughly six months for doctors at University of Kentucky Children's Hospital to nail down a diagnosis. That was also around the time Cody started having infantile spasms—a precursor to full-blown seizures—and he had a feeding tube inserted.

There are forty-six chromosomes in the human body. A typical person has a pair of numbers 1 through 22, as well as the two sex chromosomes, an X and a Y for males and two Xs for females. Wolf-Hirschhorn syndrome, which occurs in around one of every fifty thousand births, according to the Cleveland Clinic, results when someone is missing a small piece of chromosome 4—the fourth largest of the twenty-three pairs, representing roughly 6 percent of all DNA in humans.

One piece of one chromosome, and yet it can cause a litany of serious medical issues—heart defects, kidney failure, developmental disability, difficulty swallowing, seizures, cleft lip—and it can be deadly, as would be predicted for Cody.

The syndrome is named for Dr. Kurt Hirschhorn, an Austrian-born physician who first diagnosed the genetic defect in 1961, and Dr. Ulrich Wolf, a German geneticist who documented a similar case in 1965. Hirschhorn's family fled to Switzerland to escape the Nazis in 1938 when he was twelve. They immigrated to the United States in 1940, settling in Pittsburgh. Hirschhorn left the University of Pittsburgh after one semester to join the army and enrolled at New York University when he returned, earning his bachelor's and medical degrees. He started a research lab at NYU in 1958.

When Kelly and Leslie were told Cody had Wolf-Hirschhorn, they were presented with the laundry list of problems their son would face, but, as daunting as it sounded, at least they knew what they were up against.

"It was actually a bit of a relief, because we could start staring at the monster that we were facing, so that was helpful," Kelly said, providing a glimpse into the mindset he and his wife adopted from the moment Cody was born. "Then you can start educating yourself on what you're dealing with."

Despite reeling from the prospect of a lifetime of challenges facing their son, Kelly and Leslie maintained a glass-half-full outlook and resisted the temptation to ask the obvious question—Why us?—though they did wonder whether they had somehow passed on the genetic deformity.

"We have never had the woe-is-me thing," Kelly said. "I've spent a lot of time looking back. I've never done drugs or anything like that. I had my fair share of beer back in my day . . . the stuff you do when you're young. I look back and try to pin down something that I could have done to pass this along. You just have a lot of random stuff go through your head. Some of the jobs I've done. I've welded for twenty-five, thirty years, done a lot of work with machinery, chemicals. You question yourself, wondering if that could have caused it."

Like the vast majority of Wolf-Hirschhorn cases, Cody did not inherit it from his parents. But it's not as if the Dormans had the time to dwell on it anyway.

During one of Cody's hospitalizations, his parents were given a grim prognosis when a doctor at UKMC told them Cody would not live to see his second birthday.

"Just take him home," the doctor said. "Make him as comfortable as you can and enjoy him while you can."

That advice drew a defiant rebuke.

"No, that's not good enough, buddy," Kelly replied. "We're not doing that."

Even though they did not yet fully comprehend the scope of what their son was up against, Kelly and Leslie refused to simply wait for him to die.

"We weren't going to accept that without a fight, because by that point Cody had already showed us how much fight he had in him," Kelly said. "We were going to stand right there with him, toe to toe, and whatever we were up against we were going to roll with it."

After the two heart surgeries at UKMC, they took Cody to Cincinnati Children's Hospital when he was around eight months old. Ranked the best children's hospital in the country in U.S. News & World Report's 2023–2024 Honor Roll, Cincinnati Children's experiences more than a million patient encounters a year, and yet its doctors can expect to see only a few new Wolf-Hirschhorn cases, according to Dr. Robert Hopkin, Cody's longtime geneticist.

"We've been blessed to have wonderful doctors around us who have not only helped Cody, they've helped us, but we hit a few bumps in the road," Kelly said. "Not too long after his second heart surgery, I didn't appreciate how they were going about it [at UKMC]. It was almost like they were excited they had a patient with this syndrome."

There was a chance meeting one day with one of Cody's doctors in a hospital parking garage. Kelly was put off by her attitude about treating Cody. When they took him for a follow-up office visit after a hospitalization, they saw on an exam table a piece of paper and a camera.

"I need you to sign this paper," the doctor told them, prompting Kelly to ask what they were being asked to sign. It was a release form.

"What am I releasing?" he asked.

"I'm doing a paper that I'm going to publish on Cody and the syndrome, and I need you to sign this so I can publish it," she said, adding she wanted to take pictures of him from head to toe.

To the Dormans, it seemed as if the doctor's priorities were askew.

"I told her I was more interested in her treating my son than publishing a paper and taking pictures," Kelly said. "And she got mad about it. We kind of had a few words back and forth and I said, 'I'll tell you what, I'm going to put a stop to this right now. I want all of his records.'"

Like Bill Belichick and the 2014 New England Patriots, the Dormans were on to Cincinnati. Soon after they arrived at Cincinnati Children's, they were referred to Hopkin, one of the leading geneticists at the hospital. He laid out a game plan for treating Cody that would require a team effort. Hopkin was the quarterback.

"You're going to be involved with a cardiologist, neurologist, kidney doctors, feeding teams," Hopkin told them. "Basically what I'm going to be through this whole thing is the hub of this big wheel, and everything is going to go through me, and everything's going to be coordinated."

According to Hopkin, who came to Cincinnati Children's for a fellowship in 1994 and never left, the prediction that Cody wouldn't live to be two was not far-fetched.

"A significant number of Wolf-Hirschhorn patients will die in the first year or two of life," he said. "They have difficulty with growth, feeding, malnutrition. And if those things can't be managed successfully, then

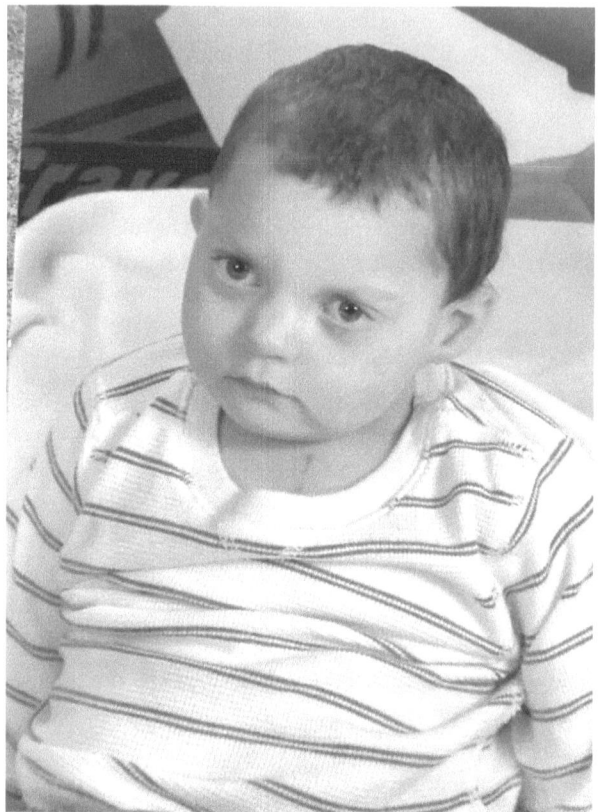

Cody beat the odds from the time he was born.
DORMAN FAMILY.

they will die young. That is fairly common. And then you have the kids who make it past that period who will live longer. Some of them will live well into adulthood."

Hopkin recalled his first meeting with Cody.

"I think he was about eight months old. I did not make the diagnosis. Somebody else did at another institution," Hopkin said. "But they came here for some feeding management and airway issues, and I met them. He was tiny and frail looking and he had some surgeries by then and would need more. When I met them and I talked to the family, they were very concerned, wanted to do whatever was needed to provide him with the best life, but they were also worried that they didn't want him to be constantly in the operating room. And how do we balance these needs? That's always tricky."

The Dormans were fortunate to find Hopkin, who helped rebuild the hospital's Human Genetics division founded by Dr. Josef Warkany, a pioneer and leading expert in the study of prenatal health and birth defects. Warkany (like Hirschhorn, an Austrian-born physician whose family came to the United States as Nazism started to take hold) had established a fellowship in genetics, but it had been inactive for at least ten years when Hopkin arrived in Cincinnati.

Hopkin did not plan on studying genetics, but a traumatic experience in medical school set him on that path. He grew up in Indian Springs, Nevada, the closest town to a nuclear weapons test site, and near Area 51, a highly classified US Air Force installation some conspiracy theorists believe the government uses to store fallen UFOs.

When Hopkin was growing up, most of the people in town worked at the testing site or air force base. There was no health care available in the town.

Initially, he left for college at Brigham Young University in Utah and majored in zoology. "I was very interested in wildlife and I wanted to go out and study animals in their habitat," Hopkin said. "Then I found out that nobody pays you to do that. So I had to find a new way to make a living. I went to medical school with the idea that it would give me four years to figure out what I wanted to do."

As a third-year student at the University of Nevada Medical School in 1990, Hopkin came across two babies born with severe chromosomal abnormalities. The obvious move was to call in a geneticist. To his surprise, that was easier said than done.

"The only geneticist in the state was on vacation, and these two kids just got sicker and sicker and sicker and died," Hopkin said. "I thought that was terrible. So I asked, 'Who takes care of these kids?' And the neonatologist said, 'Well, genetics usually meets with them and gives them the diagnosis, but they can't change anything. But they do take the heat off of us because we don't have to give the bad news.'"

Hopkin told himself, "I need to learn how to have those conversations."

That led to a rotation in genetics, and after Hopkin had an opportunity to see what a difference a doctor can make when discussing a difficult diagnosis with a family, he found his calling, even if he wasn't fully aware of it.

Hopkin trained in pediatrics at Phoenix Children's Hospital and Maricopa Medical Center in Arizona, having come to the realization that he would prefer to treat younger, lower-maintenance patients. "Adults want to complain a lot but not make any changes," he said. "I liked kids because they want to play and they want to be happy."

Hopkin started staying late to visit children with genetic issues, prompting his advisor to suggest a fellowship in genetics. "Fellowships are for researchers. I don't want to be in a lab," he told her.

The advisor persisted, telling him there was a need for doctors who had the skill and will to take care of these patients. And then Hopkin, too, was on to Cincinnati, after convincing his Arizona-born wife it would be a temporary move.

"I told her we can stand anything for two years," he said.

Two years had turned into fifteen by the time the Dormans showed up with Cody, a typical Wolf-Hirschhorn patient for Hopkin.

"He started off pretty average, and I was worried about that because the average kids have a lot of problems," Hopkin said. "He did have risk for aspiration, airway problems, feeding problems, very poor growth, and even if we put in a G [feeding] tube, inability to put in enough calories and nutrients to keep him healthy. When we start to see those problems coming up again and again, a lot of the kids just aren't able to overcome that."

As he discussed his history with Cody on an April afternoon in 2023, Hopkin was pleased to be talking about his patient in the present tense.

"I've been really happy with how things have gone with him because he did get past those early problems," Hopkin said. "And if you get through that critical early childhood part, then your ability to be treated for and to recover from those kinds of events gets better, as long as you haven't developed any permanent lung disease or other related problems."

Hopkin also saw Cody as a fighter, and his experience told him that having equally competitive parents in his corner was critical when it came to tackling a disease such as Wolf-Hirschhorn.

"Some of the kids just seem to get through things better and we term that a fighter," Hopkin said. "I don't know that they're consciously trying to fight, but they cope with the stress better. A key element of that is the people who are providing the daily care. In Cody's case, if his parents didn't have the endurance and resilience to go through this with somebody who's got some pretty severe limitations, to pay attention to all the details to successfully manage this, he might have had a different result."

There is no secret sauce when it comes to being a parent of a Wolf-Hirschhorn kid. It is a twenty-four-hour job that comes with love, sweat, and tears.

"It's interesting because the families of kids like Cody, a lot of times they talk about how much they learned and how it's enriched their lives and they see things in a more positive way," Hopkin said. "Looking at it from the outside, it's a grind—mental and emotional—but it's also physical because if you've got somebody who is prone to aspiration and having respiratory problems, somebody has to make sure they're safe at night. So you get interruptions all the time. You make sacrifices. The parents end up doing things that they never imagined they would be able to do. They get good at the medical procedures that he needs: suctioning, chest compressions, running the feeding tubes and the feeding pumps, whatever he needs. They become experts on that kind of care."

The Dormans approached their tribulations with the ethos ingrained in them growing up on farms: They rolled up their sleeves and went to work.

"It's a lot of care," Kelly said. "He's constantly monitored, even when we're asleep."

For Kelly and Leslie, having Cody was akin to being parents of a newborn—at all times.

"Cody's always slept with a pulse-ox monitor on his toe," Kelly said. "So if anything happens, it will set an alarm off. He's had that for seventeen years. We keep a camera on him all the time when he's in his room."

Whenever Cody's oxygen saturation level dropped below 87, the alarm went off.

Then what?

Leslie looked at Kelly and smiled.

"I have to get up?" she said, part declarative, part interrogative. "Usually, he says, 'His monitor is going off.'"

Listening to Kelly and Leslie and watching them interact, it became obvious that caring for Cody was very much a two-person job.

"We just check to see what his issue is," Kelly said. "It might be any number of things. He's had a lot of bouts with pneumonia and things like that. Usually when he comes down with pneumonia, we keep him on oxygen. If his levels drop, we'll . . . keep him pumped up to where he needs to be."

Hopkin was asked whether he would have expected to one day be talking about a seventeen-year-old Cody.

"No," he said. "Actually, when he was born, I had a couple of other kids that were in a similar situation and I was worried about all of them. The other ones are not around anymore."

Cody was proving to be a survivor, though the terrifying twos awaited.

Open Heart, Take Two

Cody had just turned two when he became very ill in January 2008. Adding to the angst for his parents, his doctors at Cincinnati Children's were stumped as to the cause. They kept running tests that failed to produce answers.

"Gosh, those were terrible, terrible days," Leslie said. "I was getting aggravated because I thought surely they would be able to tell us what was wrong with this child. He was lifeless. He was just so weak."

With all Cody was up against, this turned out to be viral gastroenteritis—a nasty stomach virus.

More than a decade before the onset of COVID-19, the Dormans got a head start on the not-so-wonderful world of quarantine. Kelly and Leslie caught the bug and were confined to the hospital with Cody, feeling not much better than their son.

"We were both sick at the same time," Leslie said. "The doctors and nurses told us just to lie down and that they would take care of Cody."

Leslie's grandmother, Christine Andrew, died that month and Leslie could not attend the funeral. "There was nothing I could do," she said. "We were all in quarantine."

The Dormans had no idea the stomach virus would be the least of their problems that year.

It had been months since Cody had seizures, to the point that Kelly and Leslie were hoping this issue might be in the rearview mirror. Those hopes were dashed, quickly and violently, when Leslie walked into Cody's bedroom one day to the sight of her tiny boy's body thrashing and his eyes rolled back in his head.

Cody was having a grand mal seizure.

"I think it was the most horrible thing I had ever seen," Leslie said. "There are so many different types of seizures, but that's the one that puts the fear of God in you. It's not pleasant to see anybody go through that, especially your own child."

Now known as a tonic-clonic seizure, the grand mal—from the French phrase meaning "great illness"—causes strong muscle movements on both sides of the body, according to the Cleveland Clinic. Tonic-clonic refers to the two phases of the seizures: widespread tensing up of muscles in the arms and legs, followed by convulsions.

The Dormans, living in Georgetown, Kentucky, at the time, were told to call 911 for any seizure that lasted more than seven minutes. That happened with such frequency that the EMTs held regular meetings with hospital staff to ensure that Cody received the best care possible.

"We really appreciated that they were working to be that prepared," Kelly said. "We were frequent fliers. I don't know if every place does that, but they did. We were thankful to have professionals like that so close."

Over time, doctors prescribed Cody one seizure drug after another. There was a chart on the back of the door in the neurologist's office that listed every medication used for seizures. Cody took every drug on the list. When they exhausted domestic options, they looked abroad.

"There was a medication in Europe that was pretty effective for kids with seizures, but it wasn't approved in the United States," Kelly said. "Somehow, I don't know how it worked out, but they got approval for Cody to take it, so he was on it for a while."

Kelly and Leslie had taken CPR classes when she was pregnant, and that training would come in handy more than once.

"All his muscles tightened up and he couldn't breathe," Kelly said of one incident. "I was doing something and I remember her screaming for me. I ran in there and he was turning blue. We kept oxygen tanks around the house. I didn't freak out. I knew if I did, I wouldn't be able to do what I needed to do. I told her, 'Go get the oxygen now.' As soon as I got it on him, I just cranked it up. And I told her to call 911. That happened twice, but by the time the ambulance got there, we kind of had him back."

To further complicate matters, Cody was considered a "hard stick," his veins an elusive target for nurses trying to start an IV. During one seizure incident, the local hospital could not get the IV going, so they sent him to Cincinnati Children's. Even at one of the best children's hospitals in the world, they struggled to get the line in.

"We went to Cincinnati without an IV, which was kind of a risk because there were different drugs that can cool him off pretty quick when he's having a seizure," Kelly said. "Cincinnati had a vascular team that came in with these special lights that show the veins, and they specialize in it. This is what they do. And some of the best nurses they had couldn't do it. I think they even brought a doctor in. He couldn't do it. They had one guy that was really good. He flew on medevac helicopters, so they called him. And he came down there, and he actually got it in pretty quick."

Eventually, they placed a PICC line in Cody's upper chest, near his heart. The idea for the PICC line came from the people treating Cody through Daniel's Care—a program providing hospice care to pediatric patients diagnosed with a life-threatening illness. Despite the connotation of the word "hospice," Daniel's Care was not necessarily intended to offer end-of-life treatment.

"It wasn't like that," Leslie said. "We had a nurse and we got a lot of his medical supplies through them. We had a social worker and a chaplain who came to the house about once a week."

Daniel's Care was named for the son of Joanne and Rick Pitino, the former University of Kentucky and Louisville basketball coach. In 1987, the year Pitino and Providence College (led by point guard Billy Donovan) advanced to the NCAA Final Four, Pitino was on the way back to Rhode Island from the Big East Tournament in New York when he got the call that six-month-old Daniel, born with a congenital heart defect, had died. Daniel spent almost five months in the hospital but had come home two weeks earlier.

Cody received services from Daniel's Care until he was three. At that point, he had defied the odds, but his third year was a real struggle. The strokes that started when he was younger were becoming more of a concern.

"The first one he had, I was at work," Kelly said. "Even though he had a feeding tube, he would still take baby food by mouth. Leslie was feeding him one day, and it was like he lost control. She could see while he was eating the right side of his face droop down."

Doctors attributed the strokes at least in part to atrial septal defect—a hole in the septum, the wall that divides the upper chambers of the heart. The congenital defect occurs in around one in 770 births, according to the Centers for Disease Control and Prevention. In Cody's case, the hole was moderate size and it did not close on its own, as sometimes happens.

When surgery is required to repair the hole, the first option is typically a catheterization procedure. Nothing would come easy with Cody, however, and there was a not-so-instant replay of when Dr. Cottrill was unsuccessful using that method when he was five weeks old, leaving another open-heart surgery as the only option.

Doctors were not cutting in line to perform the operation.

"He had had another stroke and nobody wanted to do surgery on him," Leslie said. "Here we were with this child that was having strokes, but nobody wanted to do surgery. There were a lot of questions and a lot of risks. He was fragile."

One day, they got the call they had been praying for.

"I'll never forget it," Leslie said. "I was sitting at the table, and the doctor called and said that he would do the surgery."

Then, a key caveat.

"I don't think he'll make it through it," Dr. Pirooz Eghtesady told Leslie.

In a way, that call typified the plight of the Dormans, who faced so many impossible choices over the years their name could have been Hobson.

The open-heart surgery was scheduled for Cincinnati Children's in the fall of 2008. One of the people in the waiting room with the Dormans was Hugh Withers, a preacher from Columbia, who drove three and a half hours. Kelly still isn't sure how he ended up there, but he was happy to have the moral and spiritual support.

"I was glad to see him," Kelly said. "I knew him for years and I'd spoken with him at times. That meant a lot to us, him putting in the extra effort to be there. He stayed all day, too. He didn't preach to us or anything. We prayed, but most of the time we just sat around. I think he and my dad talked a lot about woodworking and he was just like one of the family being there. It helped calm the nerves a lot. I really appreciated him doing that."

When Cody had his first open-heart surgery at five weeks old, the Dormans were told he had a 75 percent chance of survival. This time, based on Eghtesady's initial reaction when he agreed to perform the operation other doctors had refused, there appeared to be a much higher likelihood they would lose Cody.

Kelly observed that Eghtesady looked like Rick Pitino and had a similar way of carrying himself, which he appreciated.

"Doctor Eghtesady didn't sugarcoat things," Kelly said. "He wasn't rude at all. But he told you like it was, whether it hurt your feelings or not. And I respect people that do that. We can take a punch."

When the surgery was complete and Eghtesady emerged from the OR, his report was remarkably similar to the one the Dormans had received almost three years prior.

"The doctor came out and he said it was one of the easiest surgeries he'd done," Kelly said. "We really weren't expecting to hear that. He told

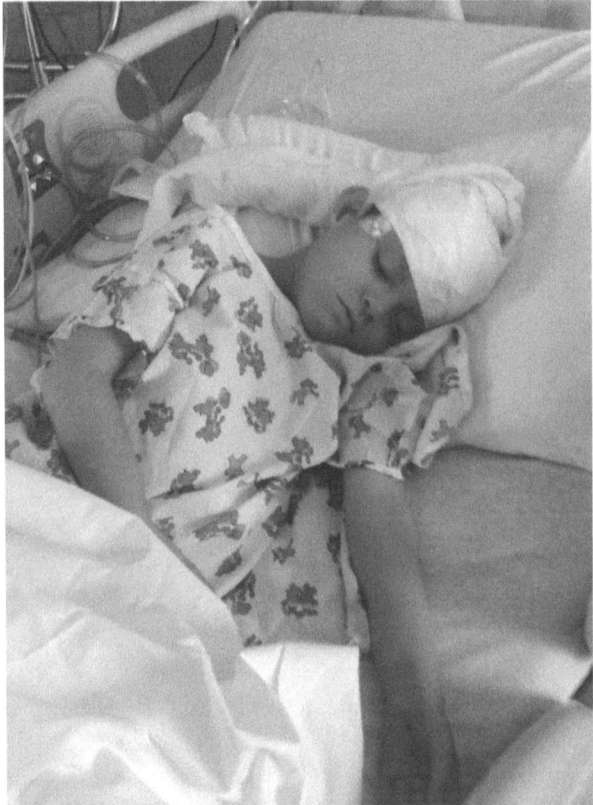

Cody's second open-heart surgery was so risky that some doctors declined to operate. DORMAN FAMILY.

us there wasn't much left to Cody's pulmonary valve at that point, after it was damaged during the first surgery to repair it."

Having dodged another bullet, Kelly and Leslie took Cody home. It would have been pie in the sky for them to hope for anything resembling normalcy, since that word left their lexicon when Cody was born. Still, was it too much to ask to go a few months without another crisis?

Apparently.

In late February 2009, Kelly was in a fishing tournament at Dale Hollow Lake on the Kentucky-Tennessee line, around 170 miles from home. It was one of his first fishing trips since Cody was born—and the farthest from home—but Leslie had all but demanded he take it. The fish were biting, and Kelly and his friend John Paul Carnes were having a grand day on the water.

Back in Georgetown, there was a problem. Cody had a gastrostomy-jejunostomy (G-J) feeding tube placed into his stomach and small intestine. The "G" section is used to vent the stomach for air and/or drainage, as well as provide an alternate way for feeding. The "J" portion is used primarily to provide nourishment, according to Cincinnati Children's.

The G-J tube was backing up, causing Cody to become lethargic and regurgitate the formula that he received through the tube. That told Leslie there was a major problem. She tried to reach Kelly, who was surrounded by water and trees, but not cell towers.

"I just went down there to fish for the day and I was coming back," Kelly said. "There was a part of the lake where you didn't have cell service or it was really spotty. We were just going to fish there for a little while and then come back. I had checked my phone, which was basically a paperweight once I got down there. I said, 'Let's just go back down to where we know we have phone service and fish there.' We got to a point in this creek maybe fifty yards wide and my phone rang."

The ringtone indicated it was Leslie. The connection might not have been clear, but her urgent message was: *You need to get home. Now.*

"I don't call when he's fishing unless there's an emergency," she said.

A breathing but unresponsive Cody qualified.

Kelly's friend pointed the boat toward land. When they arrived at the ramp, Kelly jumped off, leaving all his equipment behind, and ran toward his truck. His journey home should have been slowed by the snow and ice, but instead he managed to shave an hour off the three-hour trip.

The doctors at the local hospital couldn't pinpoint what was wrong with Cody, and they were sufficiently concerned to order a transfer to Cincinnati Children's. The weather grounded a helicopter, so they had to go by ambulance, a trip Leslie called "the scariest ride I have ever had in my life." Kelly made it back just in time to follow in his truck.

By midnight, Cody was diagnosed with a bowel obstruction and required emergency surgery.

"They knew right then that they had to open him up to see what was going on," Kelly said. "The surgeon came in about two in the morning and he was asking us all these questions. They were thinking that the J-tube that runs into his intestines had broken and punctured through his stomach or his intestines. And the doctor told us up front, the surgery would not be that difficult. We didn't have to worry about the surgery, but if he was right about what was going on, in the coming weeks Cody would go septic, which would likely kill him."

The doctors cut into Cody's stomach and had to pull out his insides, straighten them out, and put them back in. The surgeon emerged with good news. Luckily, the feeding tube wasn't broken. Cody's intestines had somehow got twisted. In a way, this was a little bit of a blessing, because the doctor discovered that Cody's intestines were so rearranged that his appendix was actually on his left side. He told Leslie and Kelly he took it out, because if Cody had an appendix rupture, it could have killed him.

With the surgery taking place in the wee hours in Cincinnati, Kelly and Leslie found themselves in an empty waiting room.

"It had always been full when we were there," Leslie said. "That night we were the only ones in the waiting room. The room seemed like it was a whole lot bigger. We could speak to each other. It was just a different feeling that night."

It was a rare quiet moment for a couple who welcomed the temporary isolation—even if it took an overnight surgery on their son to provide it.

5

Call for a Pizza?

KELLY DORMAN AND LESLIE SPOON GREW UP ON FARMS ROUGHLY FIFTEEN miles apart in Columbia, Kentucky, forty-five miles north of the Tennessee border. Kelly played football and basketball and was a shot-putter at Adair County High School, but he eventually focused on football, where, as an all-star offensive lineman and linebacker, he drew some college interest but no full scholarships.

"Western Kentucky University recruited me pretty hard," he said, "but I didn't have a full-ride offer."

His prowess on the gridiron was not the only skill that attracted colleges. Kelly was a talented artist, to the point that a few schools offered him an art scholarship. He enjoyed drawing but couldn't see himself as an art major, even though he could have used the financial assistance.

His father, Fred, is a native of Clarksville, Indiana, just across the river from Louisville, and his mother, Pat, has been in Columbia her entire life. Before they retired, Fred was a prison guard and Pat worked at the same bank for fifty years. Kelly's parents divorced during his senior year of high school in 1988 and remarried a few years later. It wasn't the easiest of times for Kelly or his younger brother, Kevin (more commonly known as "Weazer").

Kelly, born in Louisville in 1970, stayed home to attend Lindsey Wilson College in Columbia, which did not have a football team at the time. (The school has since developed into an NAIA [National Association of Intercollegiate Athletics] contender, advancing to the national semifinals three years in a row, 2019–2021.) "That's the first year I ever went to school without playing sports," said Kelly, who left after one year and started working full-time.

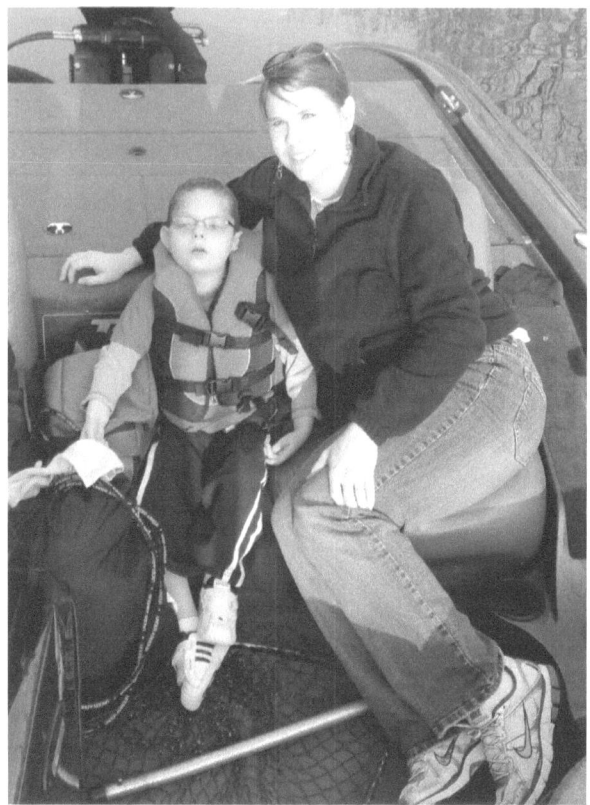

Cody enjoyed any time he got to spend with his family on the water. DORMAN FAMILY.

In addition to team sports, Kelly loved fishing from an early age, and it developed into a passion he would pass on to his son. Despite Cody's medical challenges, they found ways to spend many days out on the water, and Kelly isn't sure what Cody enjoyed more: reeling one in or providing constructive criticism on his father's technique.

"Cody loved to tell me what I was doing wrong," Kelly said. "I'd be fishing a tournament and he would send a message telling me to use different bait. He really enjoyed that."

Leslie, born in 1977, was a farm girl through and through, taking agriculture courses at Adair County High School as a member of the class of 1996. She stripped tobacco and tended to whatever else needed to be done on the farm owned by her parents, Lester and Julita Spoon. In addition to maintaining the farm, Lester was a factory worker.

Leslie had a soft spot for animals from the time she was a little girl. Her dad had a favorite horse named Bill who once developed colic—a painful stomachache—and lay down in the field. It was obvious the big saddle horse was too uncomfortable to stand or move, so Leslie reclined beside him until he finally got up and went back into the barn.

"That was his baby. He thought a lot of Bill," Leslie said. "He did trail riding with him and he always bragged about Bill. You could leave him untied and he would just follow you around. He was a really good horse. Cody got to meet him when he was young."

Leslie developed a skill for judging cattle competitions, winning several awards for her trained eye. After she graduated from high school, she worked at a video store and then as a customer service representative for the Kentucky Farm Bureau insurance company for ten years. She attempted to go back to work when Cody was a few months old, but it quickly became apparent that caring for him would be her new full-time job.

Kelly worked with Leslie's father at one point and hung around with Bryan Feese, who is married to Leslie's sister, Angie. Kelly and Leslie's first date, July 26, 2003, was a double date with Angie and Bryan.

"She was available and I was available, and we had some mutual friends who thought we'd be a pretty good match," Kelly said. "Her sister was one of them."

When they were confirming the details for the date, Leslie asked what time Kelly would pick her up and suggested 5:30 p.m.

"How about 5:23?" Kelly said.

Not sure what to say—and what she was getting herself into—Leslie asked, "Why 5:23?"

"I'm a little bit different than everybody else," he recalled telling her. "I was just making a joke, but I think she got the point pretty quick. And nothing about our life has been like everybody else."

Kelly might have been different in some ways, but it didn't take long for them to realize they were also a lot alike. As they drove to the movie theater to see *Open Range*, starring Kevin Costner and Robert Duvall, Leslie had some questions.

"Do you smoke?"

"No."

"Do you dip?"

"No, I don't dip, either."

"So far, so good," Leslie thought, until Kelly tossed a haymaker.

"Well, I do have three kids."

Leslie tried to mask her shock. She had been given the 411 on Kelly by Angie and Bryan, and no one said anything about kids.

"I was messing with her," Kelly said. "I didn't really have any kids."

The date had gone from promising to precarious to positive within minutes.

"Right then on that first date we threw everything out on the table," Leslie said. "I remember exactly where we were at, on Route 55 North, and it was just like, 'OK. This might work.' And we talked for hours every night."

With one good date in the books, Kelly called Leslie the next day, a Sunday. Not wanting to appear too pushy, he didn't call on Monday. That was a mistake.

"Bryan gets ahold of me and asks if I talked to Leslie, and I told him I didn't want to bug her or come on too strong," Kelly said. "He told me she was worried I didn't call her. That's the only day since we first went out that we haven't talked. We've really never had a bad argument or big blowup."

Kelly lived in Georgetown, around two hours north of Columbia. The relationship consisted of lengthy phone calls during the week and weekend visits, with him making the road trip. Leslie grew to dread the sight of the black duffel bag he used to carry his clothes.

"It was rough, especially on Sundays," Leslie said. "I absolutely hated seeing that black bag come out because I knew he was getting ready to leave."

After they got married, Kelly threw away the bag.

Six weeks after their first date, Kelly and Leslie were engaged.

"I had enough foul-ups, I guess. I knew a good one when I saw it," Kelly said. "Everybody told her I had money. That probably sped everything up, but she found out that wasn't true, either."

When Kelly and Leslie were betrothed, Kelly was going on a weeklong fishing trip and thought a parting gift would be in order. He bought Leslie a flower that had a big vase with a small betta fish swimming around in it. While he was away, the fish died and Leslie panicked. What would her future husband think of her not being able to keep a fish alive for a week?

Not wanting to find out, Leslie set out with her mother on their own fishing expedition. They went from store to store until they found a similar fish.

"I couldn't tell him I killed his fish," Leslie said. "So me and my momma went looking everywhere for a fish that looked like the other [one]."

Leslie and Kelly raced to the altar less than five months after their first date. DORMAN FAMILY.

Kelly may be an accomplished angler, but he's no ichthyologist, and he never knew the difference. Leslie waited a few years to tell him about the fill-in fish, which fared much better than its ill-fated predecessor.

On December 12, 2003—139 days after their first date—Leslie and Kelly were married at Hadley Community Church in Fairplay, Kentucky. As they repeated their wedding vows, they could have never imagined how drastic the dichotomy between "sickness" and "health" would become in their lives.

After he left college, Kelly had found employment framing houses in Nashville, Tennessee. The contractor he worked for built homes for country music stars including Loretta Lynn and Waylon Jennings. He found a steadier, higher-paying job as a machinist and a fabricator, eventually landing at Toyota Motor Manufacturing in Georgetown in 1996.

After twenty-five years at Toyota, Kelly took an early retirement and moved on to a job with a defense contractor.

You don't have to spend an inordinate amount of time with the Dormans to realize they are genuine, hardworking, humble people who have never been too mindful of material goods. They were born into farm life, which requires an unfailing work ethic, along with physical and mental toughness. Those traits prepared them for caring for a child with Cody's myriad challenges.

"I never thought of it that way, but it sure has," Kelly said. "I grew up on a dairy farm, and most farmwork you're up before daylight, and a lot of times it's dark before you quit. It's hard work, but it's rewarding. Growing up like that, you have chores, you make sure you do them. You can't just hit the snooze button and say, 'I'll do it tomorrow.' There ain't no calling in sick or anything like that. You look back, I think we were being prepared."

About a week after they were married, Kelly was cutting the grass on a busy Saturday. The day got away from Leslie, and she realized it was late afternoon and she had not planned anything for dinner.

Sensing that she was worried and trying to relieve the stress from his new bride, Kelly offered what he thought would be a simple solution: Let's call and order a pizza. That drew a puzzled look from Leslie, and now Kelly was confused.

Georgetown is far from a major metropolis, but it is a big city by Kentucky standards, its population of forty thousand the sixth highest in the commonwealth. Columbia, where Kelly and Leslie grew up, is home to fewer than five thousand.

"She wanted to tell me something, but she didn't want to tell me something," Kelly said. When he finally got it out of her, Leslie, age twenty-six at the time, admitted she had never called to have a pizza delivered.

"Where we grew up, we had to drive into town to meet the pizza guy," Kelly said. "She never had anything delivered to her front door. Until I moved up there, I didn't either, but I had been there six or seven years."

Kelly explained the process to her, in as nonjudgmental a way as he could muster.

"Look, you call the pizza dude, tell them what kind of pizza you want and give them your address, and when they show up, you pay them."

"That's it?" she asked.

"Yeah, that's all there is to it."

Only recently exposed to the concept of inserting a card into a machine and watching it spit out cash, this was another revelation for Leslie.

The happy couple settled in Georgetown and lived there for thirteen years. Their daughter, Kylie, was born October 10, 2013. The nearly eight-year age difference between Cody and Kylie was not a coincidence. Between being full-time caregivers for Cody and dealing with the problems he faced, and the underlying fear of having another child with Wolf-Hirschhorn, Leslie and Kelly simply weren't ready to make that leap.

It wasn't until they went to a Wolf-Hirschhorn conference in Indianapolis in July 2012 and saw healthy siblings running around that they felt comfortable trying for a second child.

"That was huge for me, seeing families that had other kids, some of them multiple kids," Leslie said.

It was also the first time they met other Wolf-Hirschhorn patients, an experience that made them realize that even if they sometimes felt like they were living on an island, they were far from alone.

"That was a life-changing event for us and for Cody," Kelly said. "It was really good for Leslie to connect with other mothers going through this. I saw her open up a lot during that time."

Seeing the other Wolf-Hirschhorn kids and families was almost cathartic for Leslie and Kelly, who had struggled not to blame themselves, even though there was no genetic indication they had anything to do with Cody being born with the syndrome.

"Just being with those other moms was a turning point for me," Leslie said. "I always felt guilty about Cody. Even though it was nothing that we did, I still lived with that. Seeing the other moms going through it was huge."

Returning home in a better psychological state, Leslie and Kelly began to give serious thought to trying to have another child for the first time since Cody was born. They were looking for some final reassurance, so they had tests done to confirm they were not carriers and how likely—or unlikely—it would be to produce another child with Wolf-Hirschhorn. They were told there was only around a 2 percent chance.

Leslie was pregnant within a few months.

It's not easy to be the sibling of a special-needs child, especially when your big brother finds unexpected fame. But Kylie—a soft-spoken, sweet, polite girl—accepted her role like a champion.

"We couldn't have sat down and molded up a better little sister," Kelly said. "She just jumps right in there to help. We hardly ever have to tell her to do anything. Everybody just does what needs to get done. We don't have an agenda or anything. If it needs to be done, we do it."

In addition to helping with Cody around the house and getting him in and out of the family van, Kylie became proficient at injecting water into

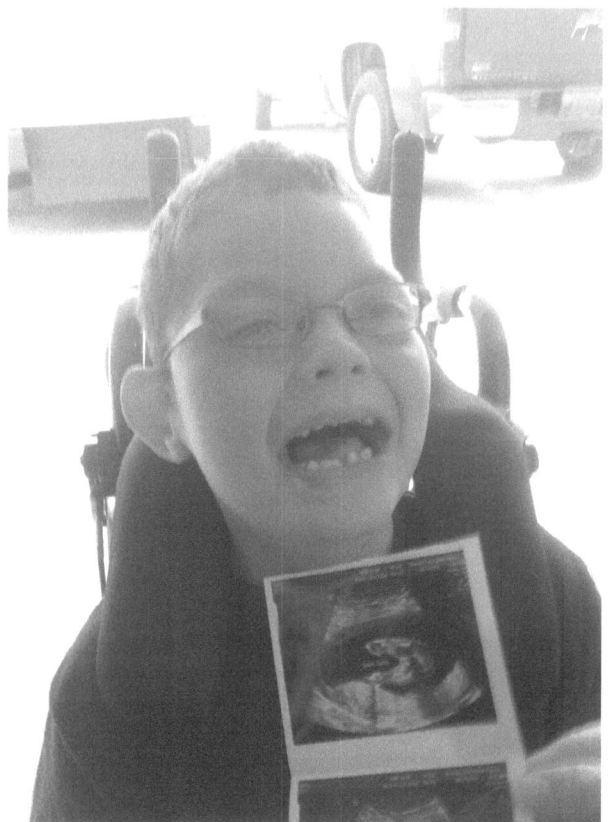

Cody was excited to learn he had a little sister on the way.
DORMAN FAMILY.

Cody's feeding tube—using what is termed the "bolus" method—in order for her brother to get the necessary hydration.

"I would help mom at night get him ready for bed and get up during the night to check on him," Kylie said.

Kylie and Cody might have missed out on many of the typical big brother/little sister interactions, but not all of them. Cody would giggle when Kylie got in trouble, adding to her sadness. Kylie knew it bothered Cody when anyone touched his wheelchair, so she had that as a means of revenge.

"He would pull my hair and sometimes I would push his chair and he would get mad and we would argue," Kylie said.

With two kids and the equipment and accommodations Cody required, the Dormans outgrew the twelve-hundred-square-foot house Kelly

Cody had a special "doctor" at home: his little sister, Kylie.
DORMAN FAMILY.

had bought before he and Leslie got married. As they searched for a bigger home, they realized they would have to relocate to afford what they wanted: bigger, one level, with a handicapped-accessible shower. They started looking in Richmond, around forty miles south of Georgetown. They would drive there to look at land and houses, and every time they checked out one particular development, off Route 75, Cody laughed, his way of offering his stamp of approval.

Kelly knew it was a stretch for them to afford to build in this neighborhood.

"I didn't think we'd be able to get in here," he said. "We just kind of nickel-and-dimed it, trying to cut corners here and there. The main thing was to get Cody's needs taken care of."

Kelly drove to Richmond one day and looked at several pieces of property, but either they were not available or he couldn't make the

Kylie was a constant presence by Cody's side. KRYSTAL MITCHELL.

numbers work. He went back to the empty lot in the neighborhood that made Cody smile.

"It's a small subdivision. Every house has about an acre," he said. "It's a one-way-in cul-de-sac. There were only about five or six houses in there at the time."

Frustrated that they had hit so many dead ends on their quest for a new home, Kelly had a come-to-Jesus moment. If that lot were still available, he would tell his friend Chad, the developer, they would take it. Then he would figure out how to afford it.

As Kelly approached the lot, he noticed the "For Sale" sign was gone, causing his heart to sink with the disappointment of another nonstarter. But as he was driving by again on the way out of the cul-de-sac, he noticed something lying in the grass. It was a sign with seven letters: "For Sale." It had been blown over by the wind.

For Kelly, it was a sign in more ways than one, and he made a beeline for Chad's office. His simple request was that his friend look at the numbers and give him the best deal possible, because the Dormans *would* be moving to Richmond.

Back home in Georgetown, Leslie had no idea any of this was going on. Kelly knew this was the plot she wanted more than anything, and with her birthday coming up in a few days, how could there ever be a better gift?

Call for a Pizza?   47

It took a while, but the Dormans found the lot they wanted in Richmond. DORMAN FAMILY.

Chad told him to come down that weekend and he would have some balloons on the lot. By this point, Leslie didn't even want to drive by. She had grown tired of getting her hopes up only to be let down. Kelly took her to a nearby subdivision he knew she wouldn't like. As they left, he told her it couldn't hurt to take a look at their dream lot one more time.

Leslie feared being embarrassed if Chad saw them drive by that land yet again, but Kelly talked her through that and off they went. There was the "For Sale" sign, upright again, with balloons tied to it. Leslie, sitting in the back seat with Cody, wondered, "Why the balloons?"

Kelly pulled over and told her it looked like somebody bought it. He opened her door and there was Chad, standing next to the sign. "Happy birthday," he said, though it took a minute for it to register that the lot was theirs.

"I got her good on that one," Kelly said. "It was pretty neat how it worked out. This is the only place Cody was happy every time we drove down and looked at it."

And the pizza man delivers there, too.

6

Life with Cody

24/7/365.

Every four years, 366.

That's the level of care Cody required, from the minute he was born and immediately rushed off to the NICU.

That was clear to Leslie and Kelly when they couldn't take their newborn home for twelve days, and when they did, he came with oxygen tanks. Virtually all parents have a baby monitor in their newborn's room; most do not have a pulse oximeter attached to their child's toe.

With Cody, the low oxygen level could be caused by any number of factors, from one of his frequent bouts with pneumonia to a full-blown seizure. Leslie and Kelly learned to live with the sleep deprivation that comes with parenting a Wolf-Hirschhorn child, and good luck trying to get them to complain.

"It's a lot of work, but he's worth it, absolutely," Kelly said, matter-of-factly. "It's never anything that we minded doing."

Some might have a knee-jerk reaction to that statement. Of course you didn't mind doing it; he's your son. The special-needs parents among us can understand at a deeper level, appreciating just what a grind it is caring for someone with Cody's level of disability.

And it never stops.

"We brush his teeth, bathe him, dress him," Kelly said. "He's been on a feeding pump since he's been about six months old, so we connect him to that."

Cody started occupational and physical therapy when he was seven months old. He was enrolled in First Steps—Kentucky's early intervention program for children with developmental disabilities. When he turned

Kelly passed on his love of fishing—and his sense of humor—to his son.
DORMAN FAMILY.

three, he entered the school system, which became responsible for providing the many therapies and services he required.

Leslie recalled bringing Cody to preschool, hoping that, despite his impairments, he could experience at least some of what that environment had to offer. That lasted one day, not because Cody couldn't handle it but due to a 2009 swine flu outbreak that would cause more than twelve thousand deaths in the country. Cody's condition made him especially vulnerable, so he was limited to learning at home. Ten years later, the outbreak of COVID-19 dictated that the rest of the country would join him. Cody was ahead of the curve.

As Kelly and Leslie dealt with the inherent challenges of caring for their child, they resigned themselves to navigating this journey primarily on their own. Cody was simply too high-needs to leave him with anyone else, including immediate family. The parents realized and accepted that, but try explaining it to grandparents, whose desire to help raise their grandchildren is part of their DNA.

"I've said it more than once," Kelly said. "We live on an island."

For Cody's parents, it was at times frustrating that not everyone could see what was so obvious to them.

"I guess people don't get it. We can't just get up and leave," Leslie said. "We can't just leave him with anybody. We've been criticized a little, because we've not left him with grandparents, especially when he was little."

You don't think the Dormans would have loved to bring Cody down to Columbia and leave him with either set of grandparents? Go out for dinner, maybe have a glass of wine or a bottle of beer? If anyone could use a break, they could. In an ideal world, perhaps, but not in their real world.

"We realized the magnitude of what we were up against way before anyone else did," Kelly said. "And it took a long time for it to really sink in with others. I think my parents had some animosity toward us for not letting them watch him. And trust me, I would have loved to have been able to do it. [But] a lot of times he would have seizures and we would know it, but nobody around us would know it."

And then there were the feeding tube, the dozens of medications, the specialized wheelchair . . .

"We never wanted anybody's sympathy or anything like that," Kelly said. "Just having understanding is a lot more important than sympathy. And sometimes we don't get that. And that's not to say anything bad about anybody. We know everyone means well."

Cody did enjoy good relationships with all his grandparents, despite living a distance away and the constraints placed on all of them by his disease.

To illustrate just how formidable a task it was caring for Cody, it was not uncommon for nurses to decline to get involved.

"There'd be some who would come out one day, see all that has to be done, and say, 'I'm not doing that.' Then we move on to the next," Kelly said. "We went through a lot of nurses like that. They just wouldn't take on that kind of load."

Someone suggested they have a nurse in the house around the clock, to take at least some of the load off them. Leslie respectfully declined.

"I'd rather just take care of him," she said, and while that was very much a two-person job and Kelly did more than his share, he is clear on who played the leading role. As far as Kelly is concerned, the Mother of the Year trophy could go to Leslie and be retired.

"She's the trouper in all of this," he said. "I take very little credit for it."

The following list—which the Dormans prepared as a cheat sheet for themselves and any nurses new to his case—illustrates how much work went into caring for Cody.

CODY'S SCHEDULE

7 a.m.
Doxazosin (Cardura)—1 tab in the J-tube (4 mg). (J-tube is on top; G-tube is on the side.)
Clonazepam—2 tabs in the J-tube.
Fluphenazine (Prolixin)—1 tab in the J-tube (1 mg).
Zonisamide (Zonegran)—6 caps in the J-tube (150 mg). (Open and mix with water.)
Primidone—3 tabs in the J-tube.
Sertraline—7 ml in J-tube.
Provent—2 puffs by mouth.
Risperidone—3 ml in J-tube.
Dantrolene (Dantrium)—3 caps in J-tube (open and mix with water).
Tolterodine—1 cap (open cap and mix with water).

When Cody wakes up
Turn off pulse ox.
Nose may have to be cleaned out. Use saline drops.
Hook up to catheter. Wash hands and wear gloves.

11 a.m.
MiraLAX—¼ cap mixed with 1 ounce of water in J-tube.
Calci Mix—1 tab in the J-tube.
Give 5 ounces of water boluses very slow in the G-tube, by gravity. Do not push it through.

Noon, 3 p.m., 7 p.m.
Hook up to catheter. Wash hands and wear gloves.

2 p.m.
Clonazepam—2 tabs in J-tube.
Cetirizine—10 ml in J-tube. (Make sure pill is crushed so it doesn't clog the tube.)

2 p.m. and 6 p.m.
Give 5 ounces of water boluses very slow in the G-tube, by gravity. Do not push it through.

6:30 p.m.
Give Cody a bath and brush his teeth.
Put pulse ox on big toe. (Use Mefix tape to make sure it stays on.)
Put diaper on with pad in diaper.
Use 2×2 IV dressing sponge around G-J tube. Use 4 pieces of Mefix tape to keep it on.

7 p.m.
Cody watches *Wheel of Fortune* on TV or DVR.
Clonidine (Catapres)—1 tab in the J-tube.
Zonisamide (Zonegran)—6 caps open and mixed with small amount of water.
Fluphenazine (Prolixin)—1 tab in the J-tube (1 mg).
Ramelteon (Rozerem)—1 tab in the J-tube (8 mg).
Primidone—4 tabs in the J-tube.
Clonazepam—1 tab in the J-tube (2 mg).
Dantrolene (Dantrium)—3 caps in J-tube (open and mix with water).
Amitriptyline—3 tabs in J-tube (30 mg).
Amlodipine—3 tabs in J-tube.

Bedtime
Hook up and turn on pulse ox. Put tape around probe to keep it on.
Tape oxygen to his face. (Only use Mefix tape.)
Hook up feeds to J-tube and G-tube with Farrell bag.
3¼ cans of Peptamen Jr. 1.5.
Lock bed at both ends and double-check.
Latanoprost (Xalatan) eye drops—1 drop in each eye after he is asleep.

"It's a huge burden," said Dr. Hopkin, the geneticist at Cincinnati Children's, noting that even the most well-intentioned parents can see their endurance wane over time, while their own relationship is prone to damage.

"Yes, it's a lot of strain," Hopkin reiterated. "We see families where they might take excellent care of the sick child, but it disrupts the relationship. We see other kids in the family feeling like they're not getting the attention that they need because mom and dad have to do everything that it takes to keep the sibling alive. It's tough. . . . Sometimes it just seems like the parents just get worn down and they can't keep up with it anymore."

Maybe it was their upbringing on farms, or maybe they are just wired differently, but if you spend any appreciable amount of time with the Dormans, you realize they were eminently qualified for the role thrust on them—which doesn't lessen the degree of difficulty.

"It's a different level of fatigue," Kelly said, "a kind of tiredness that you cannot describe. We're tired—mentally, physically, spiritually. Over time it wears on you pretty good."

Starting when he was three, Cody's teachers and therapists—occupational, physical, and speech—came to the house, first in Georgetown and then in Richmond, where the family moved when he was ten. When Cody was an elementary school student, Leslie began taking him to Cardinal Hill Rehabilitation Hospital in Lexington for the therapies, but his teachers continued coming to their home.

The teachers shared Leslie and Kelly's opinion that inside the physically ravaged body was a sharp mind. His intellectual development might have been delayed, as is common with Wolf-Hirschhorn patients, but it was clear to those closest to him that he had intelligence. The challenge would be finding a way for him to manifest it.

Identifying the right device to help Cody communicate proved to be no easy task. When he was nine, they went to the Perlman Center at Cincinnati Children's, which tried several devices without much success. Cody suffered from cortical visual impairment, a disorder caused by damage to the parts of the brain that process vision, according to the National Eye Institute. Because his ability to effectively use a tablet would be dependent on eye movements, it was a challenge.

In the fall of 2017, the therapists at Cardinal Hill recommended a ChatFusion 10 tablet and arranged for Cody to borrow one at first. He got it just before Christmas, the device converting his thoughts to spoken dialogue. A camera mounted on the tablet allows individuals to use small head movements to control the pointer on the screen and activate letters or select words and phrases.

As anxious as they were to have meaningful two-way conversation with their son, Kelly and Leslie tempered their expectations. To that point, when they were trying to evoke a response from Cody, they would hold up "Yes" and "No" cards, but even then they had to guess whether he was really looking that way. "His eyes and his brain don't work that well together," Leslie said.

They figured if they could at least be reasonably sure of Cody's choices, that would be progress. If he could use the device to tell them when something was bothering him, even better.

"Up until then, especially medically, everything was a guessing game," Kelly said. "We got really good at interpreting body language and things

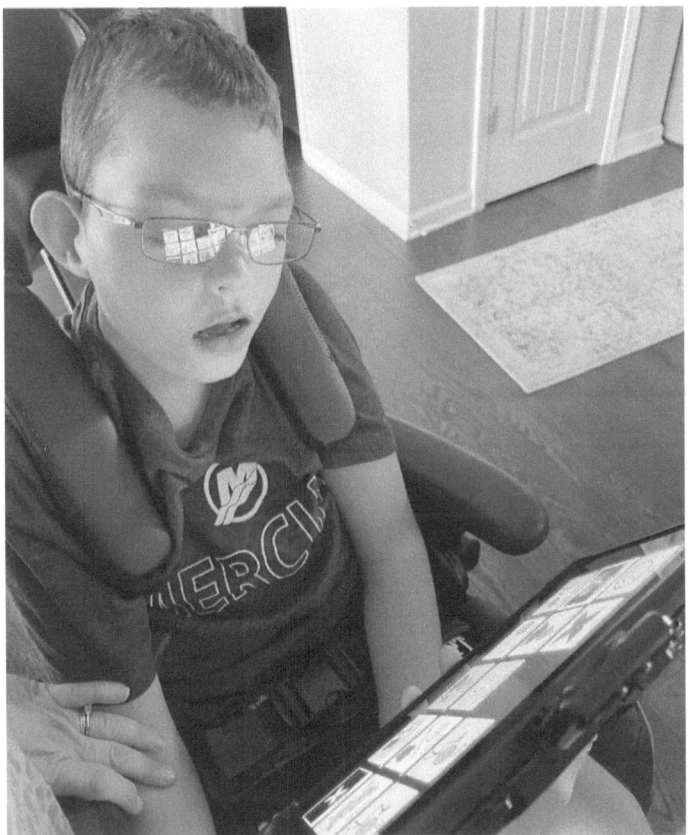

The communication tablet was a game changer for Cody.
DORMAN FAMILY.

like that, but narrowing things down was a long, drawn-out process and it led to a lot of testing when he was in the hospital, that I guess a lot of times wasn't necessary, but we didn't know what to look for. When we got the tablet, the only thing I would have asked for is him to be able to say yes or no. And if he hadn't done anything other than that, that would have been a major milestone."

They got that and so much more.

"He just took off with it," Leslie said. "He did so well with it."

After some back-and-forth with the health insurance provider, Cody was approved for his own tablet.

It was a bonus when the tablet allowed twelve-year-old Cody to tell his parents what he wanted for Christmas for the first time; he asked for the biggest iPad available.

Cody was a guest on the *HHH Racing Podcast*.
DORMAN FAMILY.

Why another tablet? Think of the ChatFusion as being for business and the iPad for pleasure.

"He could have asked for Fort Knox and we'd have tried to buy it for him," Kelly said. "We went into Best Buy and they have all the iPads lined up, from the smallest ones to the biggest. We picked out the second-biggest one and he said no. He wouldn't budge. He had to have the biggest one."

Cody took delight in knowing he was sticking his parents with a hefty price tag, laughing all the way home from the store. Kelly and Leslie exacted some revenge when it came time to open Christmas presents, making the iPad the last gift for him to open.

"He was so mad," Leslie said. "He fussed and fussed the whole time we were opening gifts, and as soon as we let him have it, he was just excited as he could be. It was just neat that he was able to pick out a Christmas present."

As Cody became proficient with the communication tablet, his parents realized how much they had been underestimating him. Not only did the tablet provide a vehicle for meaningful communication, but it also allowed him to show off his academic prowess and sense of humor.

Dr. Cameron Thomas, Cody's neurologist, recalled the first clinic visit after Cody got the tablet, when he was pleasantly surprised to have his patient use it to tell him a few "knock-knock" jokes. That piqued the curiosity of the neurologist, who came to Cincinnati from his native Salt Lake City, with a pit stop in Russia.

A Mormon who went to the University of Utah, Thomas left after one semester as a civil engineering major to serve a two-year mission in Russia. He volunteered at children's hospitals and orphanages, leading him to the conclusion that he was more suited to help humans than improve infrastructure. After graduating with a degree in Russian language and literature, Thomas went to medical school at the University of Colorado. He came to Cincinnati Children's for his residency and never left.

As he watched Cody navigate his tablet, it occurred to Thomas that one of his children who was about the same age was working on geography in school. He started quizzing Cody on state capitals and was amazed at the accuracy of the answers.

"He probably rattled off twenty different states and capitals for me right there in the clinic," Thomas said, confirming the belief Leslie and Kelly had that their physically incapacitated son was indeed an intelligent boy.

In a subsequent visit, Cody told Thomas he was annoyed because he felt his math teacher didn't know the material that well.

"Given everything he had been through, I definitely didn't anticipate when he was three that in middle school he'd be complaining to me about his math teacher," Thomas said.

More than simply giving Cody a voice, the tablet provided a vehicle for the personality locked inside his body by Wolf-Hirschhorn to escape. Leslie and Kelly knew it was in there, and it didn't take long for their son's sense of humor to shine through.

At a boat show not long after Cody got the tablet, it wasn't working properly. Kelly and Leslie tried to fix it, without success. After about ten minutes, they noticed Cody laughing—at them, not with them.

Cody had figured out a way to lock the tablet so that his parents couldn't get back into it, and he got a kick out of watching their futility. They were forced to admit defeat.

"We couldn't figure out how to get it going, so we had to give it back to him and ask him to open it back up," Kelly said. "He was laughing because he knew he did it on purpose."

The tablet's ancillary value as a practical-joke tool established, more serious benefits followed. For Cody, it was a game changer academically, allowing him to show his teachers, as he had his parents, that they had underestimated his aptitude. They had been giving him material more suited for preschool than middle school. It's difficult to fault them; because his physical disability was so pronounced, it was easy to conclude that he couldn't handle more.

There was the day a math teacher put up an equation on a whiteboard and started to explain to Cody how to break it down to get the answer. Before the teacher got too far, Cody used his tablet to announce the correct answer—so quickly that the teacher thought it was a lucky guess, but Cody had actually figured it out.

That was an indicator of Cody's intellectual capability and a foreshadowing of academic success that would have been hard to envision before the tablet.

"Cognitively, he's very smart," said Amy Godsey, a Madison Central High School teacher who started working with Cody at his home when he was a tenth grader. "He tested so high on his assessments he was studying the same material as higher-functioning kids."

In 2020, when Cody transitioned to high school, the pandemic had forced remote learning on virtually all schools. When Zoom replaced the actual classroom, Cody got something he desperately wanted—a chance to study alongside his classmates, albeit electronically.

Madison Central, the second-largest high school in Kentucky with more than twenty-two hundred students, did its best to help Cody, a member of the class of 2024, feel like part of the school community, including him on the fishing team and the Future Farmers of America (FFA) club. Leslie and Kelly won't forget the smile on Cody's face when the fishing team brought him his uniform shirt and the FFA his official jacket. They were thrilled for him to be part of teams and satisfied that their child, who had already been through more than a lifetime of adversity, had something that made him feel genuinely happy.

Leslie took on the role of advocate when it came to pushing for inclusion, especially after the tablet unlocked Cody's academic proficiency. He was waiting with her at the hair salon one day, and she started giving him some simple addition problems. Too easy. She moved to multiplication and then division. Same results.

Cody took pride in being a member of the Future Farmers of America.
DORMAN FAMILY.

"He was just popping off the right answers," she said. "I was floored."

It was time to try to quantify Cody's academic ability, so they decided to have him take the ACT, an exam designed to gauge a student's readiness for college. There are four sections of the test: English, math, reading, and science. Each subject is scaled 1–36, with the overall score being the average of the four individual marks.

Kelly and Leslie had no illusion of Cody going to college, but they felt it was important for him to have the opportunity to take part in the rite of passage the ACT and SAT exams signify. On a different assessment he had scored too high to remain eligible for special-education classes, so he was taking a regular course load.

At first, the school did not want to allow Cody to use his tablet for the ACT, which would have effectively eliminated his chance to take it. That upset Cody and angered his parents, who were not looking for Cody to receive special treatment but weren't about to sit back and watch their son get a raw deal, either.

One night after midnight they heard him crying and went to his room to check on him. When they asked him what was wrong, he told them—ironically, using the tablet—that he was upset he couldn't take the ACT. Think about that. Here was a kid at an age when many high school students dread the thought of taking high-stakes standardized tests, and he was crushed that he couldn't take it.

While Kelly Dorman presents as a gentle giant, his wife is the prototypical soft-spoken, respectful farm girl, "slow to anger" but full of compassion, as King David wrote in Psalm 145. But do something she perceives as mistreating her children, and the "slow" part of the equation disappears faster than a seal in an ocean of great white sharks.

"I think the older I'm getting, the Spoon temper is coming out of me," she said, referring to her side of the family.

Throughout Cody's life, Leslie and Kelly were beyond grateful for everyone who made a positive impact on their son, and that was a long list. They also knew their little guy—all seventy pounds of him—couldn't stand up for himself, figuratively or literally—and they were prepared to fight battles he couldn't.

The school district relented. Cody could take the ACT using his tablet and with an accommodation of extra time. He wasn't about to squander the opportunity, and in the days leading up to the exam he was glued to the iPad, watching YouTube videos of math problems.

Cody took the ACT in October 2022, and his average score was 10, landing him in the middle of the below-average range (1–16). He took the test again in March 2023, determined to do better. Yes, this was the same kid who was supposed to be dead before he turned two.

The scores arrived electronically on March 25. Leslie, who typically doesn't show much emotion, couldn't hide her joy.

With the unmistakable smile of a proud, satisfied, vindicated mom, she reported that Cody had improved his score in all four subjects. His teacher told him that students usually go up in one area, maybe two, but Cody went up in all four.

Leslie read the scores:

Subject	October	March
Reading	10	15
Math	12	14
Science	10	13
English	9	10
Average	**10**	**13**

Leslie is not an I-told-you-so person, but she had every right to feel as good as any parent whose child had improved a test score by 30 percent, let alone one for whom even making it to preschool was considered a longshot.

"He did good," she said, with a wide smile that, due to life circumstances, wasn't seen that often.

When Cody used the tablet to ask for a Christmas gift, it was satisfying, and yet, in a way, also heartbreaking for his parents, who had to wait twelve years for such a basic request.

"I mean, think about it, we all get to pick out or tell people what we want for Christmas," Leslie said, "but Cody never got to before that."

For his parents, that was the best gift ever.

# 7

Lifesaver

OF ALL THE EMOTIONS BROUGHT ON BY THE COVID-19 PANDEMIC, FEAR was prevalent, if not dominant. Maybe not at the start, when news of the disease landing in the United States sparked curiosity more than anything, but when major events such as the NCAA Basketball Tournament were canceled—leading to frustration among fans for whom March Madness is as much religion as sport—and the world was effectively sentenced to house arrest, it left many to fear the unknown, getting sick, even dying.

In Richmond, Kentucky, being even further shut off from the outside world hit hard for Cody, who already had limited human interaction. Not that he got out all that much, but he did enjoy his teachers and therapists coming to the house, especially since he had started using the communication device.

Like everyone else, Cody switched to online learning, which opened doors in the long run, but at the outset he saw it simply as another restriction placed on an already confined existence.

"He lost pretty much every interaction he had outside of us," Kelly said. "He loved doing his schoolwork and his therapy. It gave him something to focus on."

By fall 2020, Cody was in a funk, lethargic and not wanting to come out of his room. Kelly and Leslie watched their son, a model of resilience throughout his arduous life, slide into a deep depression that had taken root in early 2019 when Leslie's father died and was exacerbated by the claustrophobic isolation the pandemic thrust on everyone. Even though he saw him only occasionally, Cody felt a connection to his grandfather and identified with his free-spirit attitude.

That depressed state of mind alarmed his parents because, despite his profound disability, Cody had always shown enthusiasm in his own way.

When Cody apologized for making them spend all their time taking care of him, it was a giant red flag. They had always viewed him as the ultimate fighter, and now they sensed he was wearing down.

"Even when he was going through all the surgeries," Kelly said, "you just had this little voice in your ear, this feeling in the back of your mind, he's going to be OK, he'll pull through it because you just know his spirit and how much fight he has. To see that light start to fade was harder than anything we dealt with."

Still, Kelly was unprepared for a distraught Leslie who greeted him when he arrived home from work one day. And he was floored by what she said.

"Cody said he had done all he could do and he was ready to go," Leslie told her husband, relaying the startling news that their son, who had fought so valiantly to live for fourteen years, was ready to give up.

The Dormans had been living with the prospect of Cody dying from the moment he was born, so the mere mention of it should not have necessarily been so daunting. But the idea that their son had gotten to the point that he was ready to surrender was a real gut punch.

"Those are the hardest words you can hear, especially after going through all that we had gone through," Leslie said. "Those are strong words."

Leslie thought back to the day at the University of Kentucky Medical Center when she had felt that touch on her shoulder before Cody's first open-heart surgery. She again turned to prayer.

"The first thing I did was I sat and prayed with him, and I thought, 'The devil is not going to get ahold of him and do this to him,'" she said. "We're a lot stronger than this. Then I waited for Kelly, and that absolutely killed me to have to tell him what this child said."

For the parents, this was a role reversal from the hours after Cody's birth, when Kelly was forced to tell his wife what their newborn son was up against. Now it was Leslie delivering jarring news.

Once Kelly got his wind back, he reacted with a competitive defiance you might expect from a former football star. And if you think there is no room for tough love in a father-son relationship in which the father is six foot two, 290 pounds, and the son is a physically incapacitated seventy-pound teenager, think again.

"I got pretty pissed off about it," Kelly said. "It jerked our chain, obviously, and we started brainstorming what we could do to help him."

First came a stern conversation.

"You ain't goin' this way," Kelly told his son. "We didn't get this far with that attitude and we're not going any further with that attitude. You need to figure out a way to get over it."

Kelly thought they could capitalize on Cody's love of fishing. But in Cody's mental state, just another day out on the lake would not do it. Kelly had followed a fisherman named Clay Dyer, who was not your average angler. Dyer was born with no legs, no left arm, and a partial right arm. He started fishing as a five-year-old and worked his way up to the Bassmaster Classic, a major event on the fishing tournament schedule.

Dyer was also a motivational speaker whose videos Kelly had seen on YouTube. He started showing them to Cody, figuring that if they impacted him half as much as his dad, that could go a long way in pulling him out of his depression.

Fisherman Clay Dyer was an inspiration to Cody. DORMAN FAMILY.

"You hear him [Dyer] speak, and you want to run through a brick wall. He's had every reason in the world to quit, but he never has," Kelly said. "So we got to showing Cody a lot of videos."

More frank conversations followed.

"See what this guy here has done," Kelly told Cody. "He doesn't have any arms, doesn't have any legs. He's out here fishing. He ties knots, drives a boat, drives a truck, all kinds of stuff. He's something else."

The videos, the talks, the examples seemed to help. The Dormans didn't let their guard down, but they fought back against COVID-19 and started getting out more frequently.

Leslie considered the possibility of an animal helping snap Cody out of his doldrums, but she was thinking about one with legs and hooves, not gills and fins. What about that horse, the one that had taken an instant liking to Cody when they met two years earlier?

Leslie called Mary Bourne at Godolphin, the woman who came up with the idea of naming the horse after Cody. Would there be a chance they could visit the horse?

Bourne assumed Cody's Wish had already shipped to trainer Bill Mott in New York to prepare for his career on the racetrack. As a two-year-old in October 2020, that's where he should have been, but a series of minor physical issues had necessitated an extended stay with Godolphin's rehab specialist, Johnny Burke, based at Keeneland, so Bourne called him.

An affable Irish immigrant, Burke had worked a few years with Dr. Michael Osborne at the Irish National Stud and Gardens, an expansive facility in County Kildare where Thoroughbreds are bred and foaled. Burke then went to Australia in 1981 and worked for legendary trainer Colin Hayes at Lindsay Park, a huge operation with a few hundred mares and a half dozen stallions.

Burke ended up working on the stallion side and remained there for a few years. In 1983, he stopped in the United States for a visit on his way back to Ireland and ended up staying. He married, had twin sons, and became a citizen in 2010. After training on his own for around fifteen years, winning sixty-three races in 568 starts with almost $1.2 million in earnings, he went to work for Godolphin in the fall of 2006.

"It's quite an operation," he said one morning in his barn on Rice Road on the Keeneland backstretch. "Everything's finely tuned and every little cog in the wheel makes it all work."

Burke's experience as a trainer honed his ability to detect what might be bothering an eleven-hundred-pound elite athlete that can't talk—or use a tablet—to communicate.

"When they end up coming in here, our whole objective is to get them turned around and back out again," he said. "Rehab, pretraining, whatever issues they come in with, we get them through that and find out what level they are. Having been a public trainer, I kind of know what I would like to get at the other end."

If there's a Godolphin trainee in the United States with a physical issue, there is a good chance the horse will end up in Lexington with Burke.

"It could be a two-year-old that went to a trainer, and in two months has a setback, and they come here. Everything in North America that's under Sheikh Mohammed, Godolphin-trained, that has setbacks, they all come back here," said Burke, who had no idea what he was getting when the Curlin-sired colt arrived.

Cody's Wish joined Burke in the spring of 2020 and spent most of the rest of the year with him due to a combination of physical ailments and growing pains as the horse developed into a massive specimen.

"He had a few minor juvenile [two-year-old] setbacks," Burke said. "Some inflammation, a little bit of this, a little bit of that. He kept growing and he was a great big horse, so we just had to let everything catch up. Nothing major."

With his regular stable at Keeneland being used as a quarantine barn for international runners in the 2020 Breeders' Cup, Burke relocated his string to the Thoroughbred Training Center on Paris Pike, around twelve miles east of the track.

When Bourne called to see whether the Dormans could visit, Burke was happy to oblige. He warned her, however, that a two-year-old colt on the verge of racing bears little resemblance to a five-month-old weanling.

At that point, Burke was only vaguely familiar with the backstory. He was sure, however, that he had a strapping, full-of-himself racehorse who had already hinted at his potential, breezing three furlongs in a fast thirty-five seconds on Halloween.

"We knew he was kind of on the upper tier from what I could see," Burke said. "I'm not much for fast works, but I just love the way he did it. It got my attention. I could see this horse had a pretty good gear."

On the day the Dormans came to visit, groom Crescencio Torres brought Cody's Wish out of his stall, just as Danny Mulvihill had done two years prior. Kelly wasn't sure what to expect, but he wasn't expecting what he saw.

"It took my breath away. He was this big, gorgeous horse. Prettiest horse I had ever seen," he said. "I actually asked Johnny if he had the right horse."

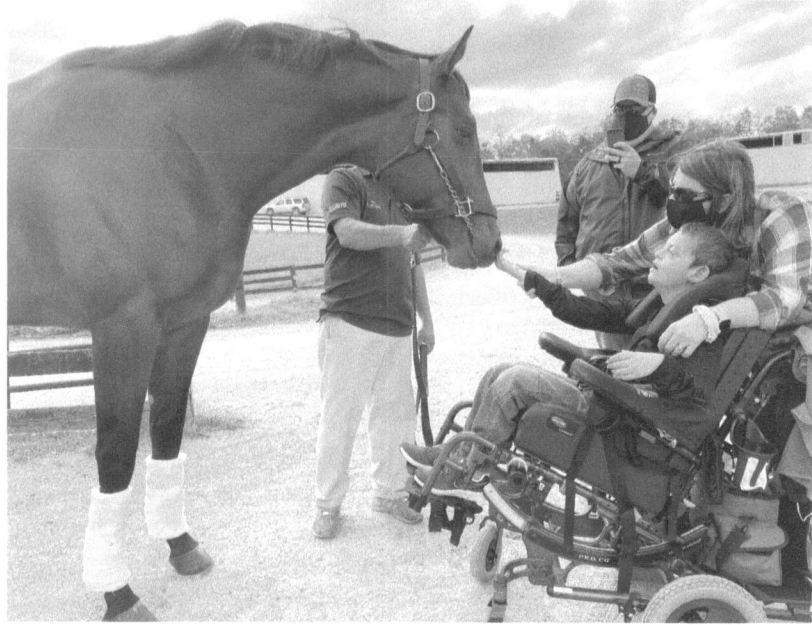

A visit to see his best friend was just what the doctor ordered to snap Cody out of his depression during the pandemic. GODOLPHIN.

Yes, this was indeed Cody's Wish.

For Kelly, this was the moment of truth. As much as he knew his son needed the psychological boost he hoped seeing the horse would provide, he had felt some anxiety as they drove the thirty minutes to Lexington. Kelly worried that the time between visits might have mitigated any connection his son and the horse established in their one and only meeting at Gainsborough Farm.

"I was a little concerned that it could backfire on us," he said. "We hadn't seen the horse in two years. In the back of my mind I'm thinking, 'The first time they met it was just a foal with a lot of curiosity. It was a neat little moment, but what are the odds of that horse even knowing who we are?'"

It didn't take long for that question to be answered.

They say true friends can go long periods without seeing each other and pick up right where they left off. On that day, in early November 2020, in the midst of a global pandemic, it became crystal clear that Cody Dorman and Cody's Wish were indeed bound to be best pals.

With Torres holding the shank, Cody's Wish showed no signs of aggression—no ears pinned back, no bucking, no neighing. When he caught sight of Cody, who was wearing jeans, black shirt, black vest, and, like everyone else at that time, a mask, it was as if no one else were there. As the horse stared at Cody, the boy began to laugh—a signal to his parents that he was truly happy, something they witnessed far too infrequently.

Cody's Wish walked over to his friend sitting in a wheelchair and once again put his head on his lap. He then lifted his head and let Cody rub his nose.

"Without Crescencio doing anything, giving him any cues, the horse put his head down on Cody's lap. I happened to be standing beside him, and the expression on the child's face was just . . ." Burke said, unable to find the words to adequately capture the moment. "I didn't realize the extent of Cody's medical issues at that point, so I got a good education on the whole thing myself. Afterwards I realized even more how significant it was because the boy was having a tough time. Watching him with the horse, it's one of those things you just can't explain."

For Cody's parents, it was mission accomplished.

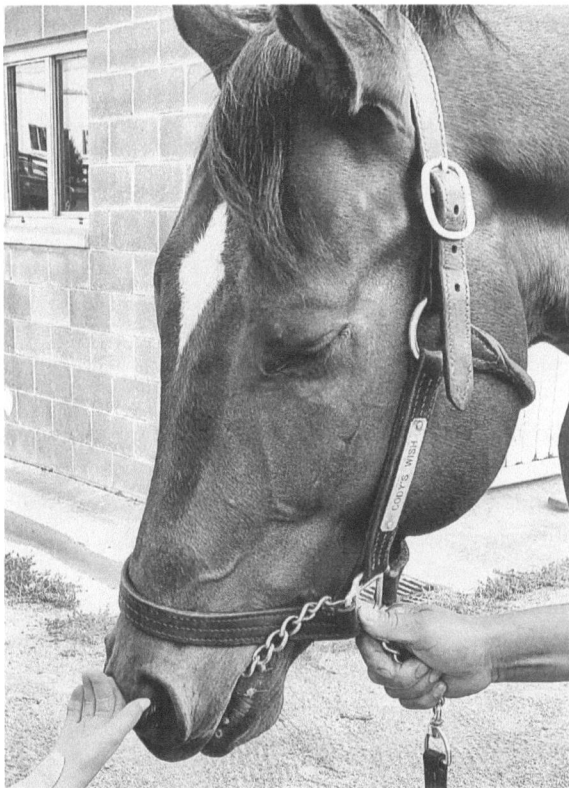

Mission accomplished. DORMAN FAMILY.

"At that minute, I knew there was something to this," Kelly said. "It was like they picked up where they left off."

Even more important than the obvious connection was that the reunion had the desired mental health effect on Cody.

"He changed my life forever," Cody said. "I feel different about things now. I'm happier."

His parents smiled, too, inside and out. They could tell their son was suddenly in a much better place, and, as strange as it seemed, they could see a burgeoning friendship.

"That was the turning point in his depression," Kelly said. "It was like we had one kid going up to the training center and we picked up a different kid and brought him back. He was laughing all the way home."

From that point on, Kelly and Leslie were sure their son had the friend he had been waiting for his entire life. He had his parents and his little sister, but they were family. Cody was desperate for a friend to call his own, and it was now clear that he had found one.

"I would tell Cody all the time, 'You and that horse, y'all got a connection. You all speak some kind of language. We can't hear it, but I know you're talking to him,'" Kelly said. "It's like the first time they met, the foal was kind of saying to him, 'Me and you are pretty cool. We're going to hang out, be buddies and stuff.'"

The second time solidified the bond.

"It's like the horse told him, 'I'm not going to let you go where you're headed. I know the path out of here, to the light or whatever,'" Kelly said.

In happier times, when Cody was reveling in the success of his namesake, he reiterated how important that day was.

"He saved my life," Cody said. "He means the world to me. He's my best friend."

The following spring, as Cody's Wish prepared for his racing debut, Kelly heard that Clay Dyer, the inspirational fisherman, would appear at a fishing tournament sponsored by a church near Columbia. Kelly knew the pastor, so he reached out and asked whether Cody could meet Dyer, even for five minutes.

As he explained Cody's situation to Brother Drew Hayes, the pastor began to cry. Not only had he experienced periods of depression himself, but he was also genuinely touched by the thought of hosting Cody. The church made Cody part of the event in what became one of his first celebrity appearances. Cody got to spend some quality time with Dyer, and a friendship was born.

Meanwhile, Bill Mott had put eleven timed workouts into Cody's Wish since he arrived at the trainer's winter base at Payson Park in Florida. Five were "bullets," meaning the fastest time of the horses who worked at that distance that day. Two more workouts were run over the Oklahoma Training Track at Saratoga, where Mott keeps horses for the seven months of the year it is open. (Located across Union Avenue, the Oklahoma got its name when riders in the early days complained it was too far away from the main track, joking that it was like going to Oklahoma to get there.)

On May 31, 2021, Cody's Wish had his final prep, breezing four furlongs in 48⅗ seconds. It was time for him to race. Mott entered him in a maiden race at Belmont Park in New York on June 4, the day before the Belmont Stakes, the third leg of horse racing's Triple Crown.

Hopes were high.

"Well, they told me I had a good one coming," said Mott, who could never be accused of overstatement. "We knew he was a big, strong horse that was well bred and then once we started breezing him, we felt he was pretty nice, you know what I mean?"

Now he had to show it on the racetrack.

8

New York Traffic

THE GODOLPHIN TEAM WAS LOOKING FORWARD TO BELMONT STAKES Weekend in 2021. Essential Quality was the morning-line favorite in the 153rd running of the "Test of the Champion," the third leg of Thoroughbred racing's Triple Crown, a grueling 1½-mile race covering exactly one lap around the expansive Belmont Park oval.

Located off the Cross Island Parkway where Queens meets Nassau County, Belmont was built in 1905 by a syndicate led by New York banker August Belmont II and former Secretary of the Navy William Whitney. "Big Sandy" saw its share of iconic horses and performances, highlighted by the immortal Secretariat, whose thirty-one-length win in the 1973 Belmont Stakes remains one of Thoroughbred racing's signature moments.

A massive structure, Belmont could easily accommodate 100,000 fans—a record 120,000 watched Birdstone upset Smarty Jones's Triple Crown bid in 2004—before it was torn down in 2024 in favor of a state-of-the-art, realistically sized facility.

Godolphin paid $300,000 in 2017 to breed its mare Delightful Quality, a daughter of Sheikh Mohammed bin Rashid Al Maktoum's Elusive Quality, to Tapit, the leading US stallion by progeny earnings the previous three years. Delightful Quality delivered a foal April 9, 2018, at Jonabell Farm in Lexington, where all but one of Godolphin's graded stakes winners in that crop were born. (The top-level races are designated by the American Graded Stakes Committee as Grade 1, 2 or 3, with 1 being the best.) Cody's Wish was foaled at Gainsborough Farm, around fifteen miles away.

Essential Quality, or "EQ" (as he was known around the barn), went to Brad Cox, one of Godolphin's go-to trainers. The colt broke his maiden in his debut race at Churchill Downs in September 2020 and went on to win two Grade 1 races that year, including the Breeders' Cup Juvenile, earning the first of his two Eclipse Awards as a champion two-year-old.

After staying undefeated while capturing two Kentucky Derby prep races, Essential Quality was the favorite in the 2021 Run for the Roses and looked like he would provide Godolphin with its elusive first Kentucky Derby win.

Of all the races in the United States every year, the Kentucky Derby is the one in which a horse is most likely to encounter trouble, with twenty horses jockeying for position from the second the gate opens. Essential Quality was the 5–2 favorite breaking from post position No. 14, with Rock Your World to his immediate right. Sure enough, there was trouble from the start, with Highly Motivated (No. 16) breaking in and forcing Rock Your World into Essential Quality. Jockey Luis Saez did a good job hustling EQ into contention, but he was caught five paths wide on the first turn and stayed wide down the backstretch.

Saez made a move on the far turn and looked like he had a chance coming down the stretch, but he couldn't get closer than fourth, losing to gate-to-wire winner Medina Spirit by just more than a length. (Essential Quality was eventually moved up to third after Medina Spirit was posthumously disqualified for a failed drug test. Mandaloun was declared the official winner.)

"He didn't get the greatest trip. He was wide around both turns," said Cox, who also saddled Mandaloun. "That can happen when you start from the fourteen hole, especially when you don't get off to a good start."

Cox opted to skip the Preakness and run Essential Quality in the Belmont, giving the horse five weeks between races. Bettors made him the favorite in a solid but not overpowering field, and the big gray horse got redemption for the Kentucky Derby loss, outdueling a stubborn Hot Rod Charlie in the stretch to win the Belmont Stakes by 1¼ lengths. Godolphin also ran 1–2 in one of the undercard stakes races, making it a super Saturday after what had been a frustrating Friday.

The day before the Belmont, the Godolphin team was very interested in a maiden race. After giving Cody's Wish thirteen official workouts over the previous six months, trainer Bill Mott deemed him ready to run. Godolphin USA chief operating officer Dan Pride and Godolphin USA president Jimmy Bell came to New York from Lexington a day early to watch the $90,000 race.

Michael Banahan, who would take over as Godolphin's director of bloodstock by the end of the year when Bell retired, called Cody's Wish "one of our top horses." In the Godolphin world, that is saying something.

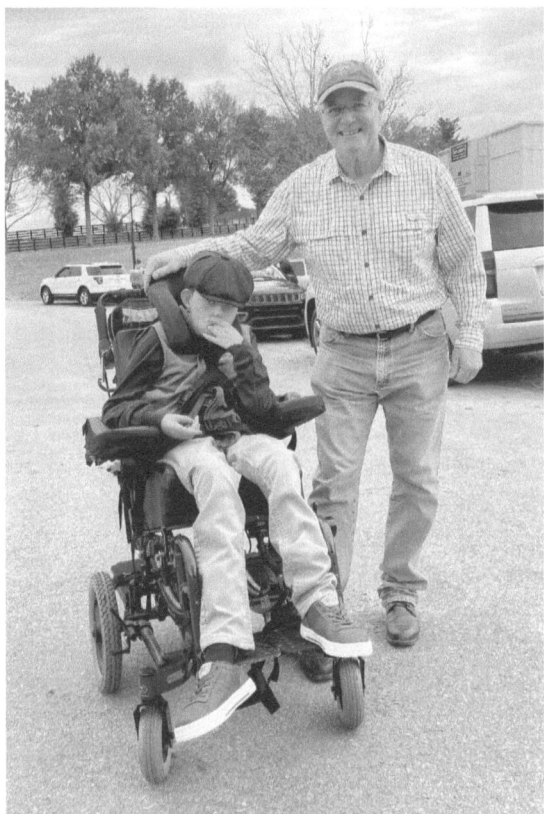

Trainer Bill Mott had high hopes for Cody's Wish from the start. DORMAN FAMILY.

Despite the optimism, there was a key mitigating factor: Mott is an old-school trainer not overly concerned with horses winning their first time out. His numbers have improved in recent years, but he wins at a lower percentage with horses making the first start of their career (around 11 percent) than with his runners overall (19 percent).

What matters most to Mott is that the horse gets an education that will prepare him to improve the next time he runs. Junior Alvarado, one of Mott's main jockeys for more than a decade, is well aware of that.

"As long as the horse gets a good experience and we teach him the right way, you don't necessarily have to win," Alvarado said. "Even if we are last and pass just one horse, the idea is to teach him how to finish, to pass horses. He doesn't want them to be close and then go backward."

Alvarado was caught off guard when Mott was atypically positive about Cody's Wish before the race.

"We really like this horse a lot," Mott told him, though he did offer a qualifier as he gave him a leg up.

"He said this might not be the right distance [seven furlongs], but you can just go with him and give him a good lesson," said Alvarado, who knew nothing of the backstory but did take note of the unusual fact that the Godolphin guys were in town for a Friday maiden race.

Back in Kentucky, the Dormans settled in front of their TV, feeling like big winners before the horses were even loaded into the gate.

"We really didn't know what to expect, but we were looking forward to it and Cody was very excited," Kelly said. "I've said many times, if that horse never ran or never won a race, him being named for Cody was a gift to us and we were very grateful for that."

It's virtually impossible to be raised in Kentucky and not have some level of familiarity with Thoroughbred racing. Still, there's a huge divide between a Sunday night drive by the farms around Lexington and watching a horse named for your son run at one of America's premier racetracks.

Eight three-year-olds lined up in the starting gate for the fourth race at Belmont Friday, June 4, 2021. Despite the positive vibes from the Godolphin camp—the type of optimism that typically finds its way from the backstretch to the mutuel windows—Cody's Wish was not the favorite, sent off at odds of 3–1.

The choice of the betting public was Mahaamel, a horse owned by Shadwell Stable and Sheikh Hamdan bin Rashid Al Maktoum, the brother of Godolphin principal Sheikh Mohammed. Sheikh Hamdan, who paid $700,000 for the colt at the 2019 Keeneland September yearling sale, had died on March 24, roughly a month before the horse made his debut at Belmont.

That sounds like—and is—a lot of money, but the Keeneland sale brings out the big spenders, with 58 of the 2,974 yearlings that September selling for more than $700,000, including 22 who went for at least $1 million. The sale topper, a daughter of 2015 Triple Crown winner American Pharoah, sold to Mandy Pope for $8.2 million, making her the most expensive filly in the history of the Keeneland September sale. America's Joy was set to begin her career on closing day of the 2021 Saratoga meet, but she fractured the sesamoid bone in her left foreleg during her final workout and died as a result of the injury.

Mahaamel finished second in a maiden race at Belmont April 24, a strong enough effort to prompt bettors to send him off as an odds-on favorite (less than even money) in the debut race for Cody's Wish.

Hall of Fame jockey John Velazquez took Mahaamel to the lead on a muddy track, while Alvarado had Cody's Wish in a battle for fourth place on the outside and encouraged him a bit to stay in touch with the leaders. Heading into the stretch turn, Alvarado made a move to stay inside of the horse in front of him, figuring he probably wasn't going to win but he might as well save some ground.

Cody's Wish had other ideas.

"All of a sudden he jumped into the bridle and took off," said Alvarado, who quickly realized he was in trouble with a horse on either side of him and a wall of three in front—the type of congestion routinely faced by frustrated drivers on the Cross Island. Cody's Wish was full of run but out of room.

"I was just trapped," the jockey said. "I didn't expect him to all of a sudden wake up like that, so I had to check [hesitate]."

Track announcer John Imbriale made note of the trouble.

"Steadying there just a bit was Cody's Wish, who has dropped back," Imbriale said from his booth high atop the Belmont grandstand. The Equibase official chart of the race mentions Cody's Wish getting shuffled back and losing around two to three lengths of ground.

Alvarado knew there was only one way out, but that required going very wide on the turn, which effectively eliminated any realistic chance he had of winning, due to both ground loss and the fact that it is not easy

Cody's Wish ran third in his debut despite a troubled trip. GODOLPHIN.

for Thoroughbreds to shift gears multiple times, especially horses as big as Cody's Wish.

Blissfully oblivious to the congestion behind him, Mahaamel enjoyed a stress-free trip and gradually increased his lead, from a half-length after the first quarter-mile to a winning margin of 3¼. Cody's Wish, meanwhile, wasn't done yet. Once Alvarado got him in the clear, he closed fast and finished third, missing second by a half-length, which might have made it even worse for the jockey.

"He came running but it was just a little too much to do at that point," Alvarado said. "I think the distance was a little bit short for him, too. He ran a pretty good third, but having to check at the three-eighths pole cost us. The people from Godolphin were expecting him to win that day and they weren't too crazy about the ride."

That might have been an understatement.

"It was just an unfortunate deal where Bill was very high on the horse," Pride said. "He had shown his talent by then. Bill had been talking about him, how much he progressed, how much he liked him. So we built our expectations, because Bill is not one to build them up. He's not touting horses left and right. So he kind of created this expectation."

The Dormans, still trying to get their heads around the idea of a racehorse named for Cody, were perfectly happy with third. The horse's namesake loved the effort.

"I think he could have finished dead last and Cody would have still been excited," Kelly said.

One aspect of the race left a lasting impression on the Dormans, especially Leslie, who pretty much demanded they watch the replay one day when Kelly came home from work. Kelly figured by that point they had already seen the race a dozen times and couldn't understand his wife's sense of urgency—until she gave him an analogy.

"Cody's Wish ran that race the way Cody has always lived his life," Leslie told Kelly. "Cody will climb a mountain, then get knocked down, but he always gets back up. That's the way Cody's Wish ran. He got in trouble, but he kept trying. That's the common denominator they have: There is no quit in either of them."

The intangible of being willing to fight through adversity notwithstanding, for Godolphin and Mott there was still the matter of what they considered a subpar ride by Alvarado.

"I'm sure Junior, if he watches the tape, he'd say, 'Not my finest moment,'" Pride said. "It was just one of those hard deals where the horse probably had a better race in him than the result shows. It happens every day."

Mott was typically measured when reflecting on the race.

"Well, he was just green," he said. "He broke a little poorly and then he was behind, so they kind of gigged him a little bit and he rushed up and, you know, once you get him started, then you can't slow him down. So he started slow and made a middle move and then flattened out is basically what it amounted to."

Alvarado was upset, but far from crestfallen. When you ride as many races as he has—more than fourteen thousand by the middle of 2025—troubled trips are part of the business. The ramifications vary, but with a Mott first-time starter, Alvarado expected some leeway.

"Normally, Bill would give me a chance to ride him back," he said. "By this point I had been riding a lot of horses for Godolphin, so I didn't know what was the big deal."

He would find out the hard way when Cody's Wish was entered at Saratoga Race Course seven weeks later. The jockey named to ride was Joel Rosario, one of the best in the country and a future Hall of Famer (inducted in 2024). Alvarado had effectively been fired.

Changing jockeys is a decision typically made by the owner, the trainer, or both. When asked about it almost two years later, Pride suggested that it might have simply been a logistical issue and perhaps Alvarado was not available that day. The charts from July 28, 2021, show Alvarado did indeed ride four races at Saratoga: Two were for Mott, one a Godolphin horse—Lake Avenue, whom he directed to a second-place finish in the Grade 2 Honorable Miss Stakes.

On the surface, it seems odd that Godolphin and Mott would ride Alvarado in a $200,000 stakes and yet were not willing to give him a second chance on Cody's Wish in a maiden race.

"I suppose it was my decision because I wasn't really happy with the way the race went," Mott said of the debut.

Welcome to horse racing.

One person not surprised was Alvarado's longtime agent, Mike Sellitto.

"When you have high expectations for a horse and it doesn't happen, sometimes it's in the best interests of everyone to do something different," said Sellitto, displaying a pragmatism that has made him a successful agent for more than two decades.

Any jockey who has ridden an appreciable number of races, even the elite, has been taken off a mount for a ride someone who matters didn't like. That's a reality, but it doesn't make it any easier.

"I won't say it didn't bother me because it did," Alvarado said. "I knew it wasn't the best first-time experience you wanted, but I didn't think it was that bad, either, to get taken off just for that. Sometimes I take it a little more personal. I knew the ability of the horse, but I also knew it was going to take him some time. Bill Mott has a way of training that they get better and better and better."

As with any significant life event, good or bad, the spouse has to live through it as well, and sometimes more vicariously than they would prefer.

In Kelly Alvarado's case, she is more than a wife when it comes to her husband's career. They are very much a team and share everything—even an X account, @JuniorandKellyA, on social media. So when adversity strikes one, the other is there for support, consolation, commiseration, you name it.

"I definitely was aware of it, because I'm the one that has to hear about it," Kelly Alvarado said. "But I feel at that point in our lives it had happened more than a handful of times and so we were used to it. It was very upsetting, but what can we do about it? We can't sit here and sulk. We just have to move on with our lives and move on with the business and just wait and see what's going to happen next."

And hope like hell for another chance.

9

Junior Achievement

WHEN RAFAEL AND NORMA ALVARADO WELCOMED THEIR SON INTO THE world May 20, 1986, in Barquisimeto, Venezuela, they decided to name him after his father. A mistake on the birth certificate, however, turned Rafael Alvarado Jr. into Junior Rafael Alvarado, and they let it stand.

His parents provided him, older brother Edwin, and younger sister Milagros with a stable upbringing that Alvarado remembers as a "great life," and he was motivated to make the most of any opportunities that came his way.

"When I was growing up, they did everything for me and my sister," he said, "and I wanted to make sure I gave them the best I could."

Rafael was a successful jockey, with Junior often tagging along. Rafael would have preferred his son join the military, but by the time he was a teen, Junior had his heart set on becoming a second-generation jockey, albeit with big boots to fill.

"If you're half as good as your father, you'll be fine," trainers would tell the kid around the barns in the morning.

After graduating from high school, Alvarado continued his education—not in college but at a jockey school in Valencia, the third-largest city in Venezuela. He got his license and rode his first winner, on a horse named Esteivana, at La Rinconada Hippodrome near Caracas, December 30, 2005—the day Leslie and Kelly Dorman brought Cody home from the hospital for the first time.

"I guess both of us had the best day we could ask for," Kelly Dorman said. "Little did we know . . ."

Alvarado moved his tack to Caracas after struggling to find mounts closer to home. He won fifty-six races in a year, and by that point his dreams extended beyond the borders of his country. Rafael had regaled him with stories about jockeys from Venezuela who were making it big in the United States—Ramon Dominguez, Javier Castellano, Eibar Coa—and told him if he really wanted to be a top jockey, he needed to go to America.

"Even though I was doing good in Venezuela at that time, it was my dream to come here," Alvarado said one morning at Gulfstream Park in Hallandale Beach, Florida, where he began his American odyssey. "My dad kept telling me about the races in the US and that I can be as good as those guys."

Alvarado started going to sports books to watch American races via simulcast. He was excited at the prospect of competing against the best, but there was the issue of immigration. His brother had that covered, finding someone to sponsor Junior for a visa.

After riding in Venezuela for about two years, Alvarado made the fourteen-hundred-mile trip to south Florida in early 2007, recording his first US win at Gulfstream on February 17, on a horse named Satira. He won eighty races at Gulfstream and Calder Race Course near Miami, and he planned to stay on that circuit in 2008. However, when he got a call asking him to come to Arlington Park, a regal facility just outside of Chicago considered one of America's most beautiful racetracks, he did not hesitate. The decision would pay off professionally and personally.

Born and raised in Chicago, Kelly Short was a high school math teacher. Her older brother, Tommy, who owned horses at Arlington, invited her to come to the races one day after school to see one of his horses run. The jockey was Junior Alvarado, and the horse did not win.

"No big deal," was Kelly's recollection, fifteen years later, although she and Junior did subsequently connect on Facebook. After about a week of communicating virtually, they decided to meet for a drink at Rosati's, a popular pizza place in Schaumburg, in the Chicago suburbs.

There was a dynamic they hadn't given much thought to and one not often encountered on a first date: Junior didn't speak English and Kelly didn't speak Spanish. At least they weren't going to argue.

"We just sat there, hysterically laughing at each other because he barely understood me and I didn't understand him at all," said Kelly, who quickly figured out that someone had been using a translation app during their online chats.

"She was speaking in English, but I didn't know what she was saying. I would say the same thing back in Spanish, and she didn't know what I was saying," Alvarado said. "We were just looking at each other and laughing."

For a guy who rides thousand-pound animals going forty miles per hour for a living, Alvarado was nervous before that first date.

"It was pretty nerve-racking," he said. "She was worried about her brother finding out she was dating me or she was hanging out with me. I was scared to death. I didn't know what to expect."

When Kelly's brother showed up at the restaurant, it added a level of angst, but while Alvarado grew closer to Kelly over the coming months, he also developed a bond with Tommy, who became a sounding board and trusted confidant.

"He was just an unbelievable person," Alvarado said. "We became very close. We just clicked. He liked horses, and we had that connection. I didn't think I would have another brother, somebody so close to me. I never talked to anyone about things that happened in a race or anything like that. I kept that to myself until he came along. He was like my psychiatrist. He was always that person for me."

As they continued dating, Kelly taught English to Junior, who proved to be a good student, his grasp of the language steadily improving. Not only was there the obvious benefit of being able to communicate with his girlfriend, but it also helped his relationship with trainers.

If you're assuming Kelly Alvarado has become proficient in Spanish, not quite.

"He still hasn't taught me Spanish," she joked. "I told him, 'If I teach you English, you have to teach me Spanish.' I'm still waiting."

Years later, happily married with three children, it is still a source of good-natured ribbing between the couple.

"I tell him he only wanted to date me because I was a teacher and he needed somebody to teach him English," she said.

It might have taken some time for Alvarado to pick up the language, but his riding ability translated just fine. He was the leading rider at Arlington in 2009 with 110 wins and finished second in the standings in 2010. He won his first Grade 1 on August 21, 2010, with Eclair de Lune in the Beverly D. Stakes, an especially meaningful victory because the horse was owned by Arlington Park owner Richard Duchossois and the race was named for his late wife.

"That was a big story and I was lucky to be part of it," said Alvarado, who had no idea that even more heartwarming victories were in his future.

The success at Arlington left Alvarado feeling confident he could be successful in American racing. The Grade 1 win prompted him to head to New York and try to make it on the country's most competitive circuit. Alvarado subscribed to the theory put forth by songwriters John Kander and Fred Ebb in their classic Empire State anthem: If you can make it in New York, you can make it anywhere.

A language barrier was no problem for Kelly and Junior Alvarado. KELLY ALVARADO.

It took Alvarado just four races to land in the Aqueduct winner's circle as a full-time New York jockey, guiding Preachintothedevil to a maiden win November 6, 2010. Alvarado won seventeen more races at the Big A, giving him 132 for the year—his best to that point.

His relationship with Kelly burgeoned too, but not to the point that the Midwestern girl was ready to move to the East Coast.

"I was born and raised in Chicago," she said. "When Junior moved to New York, I stayed back. I'm like, 'Oh well, good luck. I'm going to stay in Chicago because that's where my family and friends are, and I'm not leaving the only thing I know.' I figured he'd be back."

As Alvarado established himself on the New York Racing Association (NYRA) circuit, it became apparent that he would be there for the foreseeable future, so Kelly had a decision to make.

"He ended up having so much success that I figured I would go there for six months," she said. "I made him keep the house that we had in Chicago. Then we got to the point that we were paying two mortgages. So, I came here. And I am still in New York."

The couple became parents when son Adrian was born late in 2010. Though they were never formally engaged, they talked about marriage, giving Kelly the opportunity to have some fun with her boyfriend's immigration status.

"I would always joke that he just wanted to marry me so he could get his green card," Kelly said. "I obviously knew that wasn't the case, but I kept telling him, 'We're going to wait till you get your green card.'" Alvarado checked that box in 2013.

On December 10, 2013, Kelly and Junior, accompanied by Adrian and a friend of Kelly's, went to a New York courthouse and were married. Kelly has never regretted missing out on a formal wedding.

"It was a spur-of-the-moment thing and I have no regrets, because I hated the thought of having to spend money on a big wedding," she said. "At that time it wasn't practical for us. I still wouldn't have done it any other way."

Through the birth of two more children (daughter Adalyn in 2015 and son Axel in 2019), the highs and lows every jockey experiences, and the inevitable injuries, Kelly has been in stride with Junior. Being the wife of a jockey takes the matrimonial and matriarchal degree of difficulty to new levels.

"I know most people will say they want to separate work and family life, and for the most part Junior does, but it's hard when riding is his life," Kelly said. "He wakes up and works horses. He comes home and changes, then he goes and races. Weekends and holidays, that's where he's at. And so a lot of the times that's where we are as a family. We'll travel with him if the kids don't have school. It's easy to be wrapped up in the business, too. I do enjoy being a part of it and being able to have these experiences with him, but it comes with a lot of hardships."

At the top of that list is the ever-present danger every time a jockey gets a leg up on a horse. There is a saying in racing that illustrates the inherent risk: It's the only job where an ambulance follows you around. Indeed, if you watch a horse race, you will notice a "bus" (as they call it on the TV cop shows) trailing the horses and jockeys around the track, ready to scoop and treat a fallen rider.

Every jockey suffers injuries, ranging from dust-yourself-off to fatal and everything in between. In 2023, Alvarado received a sportsmanship award named for Mike Venezia, a New York jockey who died from injuries suffered in a spill at Belmont Park in 1988.

Alvarado has had his share of unwanted time off, thanks to four shoulder surgeries, two broken backs, three broken collarbones, and a broken ankle. Fortunately, he has made it back every time.

"I do love horse racing," Kelly said, "but I watch just to make sure that he crosses the finish line in one piece."

10

Winning Formula

When Junior Alvarado was taken off Cody's Wish after the trouble-filled first race, the only injury he had to deal with was a bruised ego, but jockeys deal with being fired every day. There are times when it's not worth a second thought, but in this case Alvarado resolved to keep track of this huge horse he believed had the talent to match.

He was vindicated to a degree when Cody's Wish lost his next two races, both at Saratoga with Joel Rosario in the irons. Trainer Bill Mott stretched him out to 1⅛ miles for his second start, and the public sent him off as the odds-on favorite. When the gate opened, he bobbled and was immediately last in the field of nine, but Rosario passed two horses entering the first turn, saving ground on the inside.

As they began their run down the backstretch, Cody's Wish was still seventh under a tight hold, but, just like the debut with Alvarado, he wanted to do it on his own terms and was very keen to run on. By the time they cleared the halfway point of the race, he was still on the inside and vying for the lead with Pipeline. Cody's Wish put his head in front on the turn but was passed by Pipeline as they straightened for home. Vindictive eventually passed both of them, and Cody's Wish had to settle for a well-beaten third.

"We were really happy to get the mount," Rosario said, referring to his agent, Ron Anderson. "He was a horse with a lot of talent, and he was amazing. I remember when we got to the gate, he was still a little bit green. But he was a very beautiful-looking horse, very long shaped, and we were really happy."

Start number three came on closing weekend at Saratoga in 2021—a seven-furlong maiden race in which Cody's Wish was again bet down to heavy favoritism. He was fractious in the gate—a harbinger of races to come—and again dead last in the first hundred yards. Rosario started to advance on the rail and then took Cody's Wish to the far outside coming off the turn, as Pipeline—a familiar foe who would play an important role in his future—took the lead in the stretch. Cody's Wish lost a battle for second with Waxman.

Three races in New York, three losses for a horse with seemingly limitless potential. The Godolphin team was disappointed, but far from ready to give up on the big boy.

"I think in those races, circumstances just conspired against him," Michael Banahan said. "He didn't break exceptionally well, so things just didn't work out. But at the same time, he ran against some decent horses at Saratoga, which is unusual for three-year-old maidens at that time of the year. A lot of the good ones are gone at that stage [having won and advanced beyond the maiden ranks]. When you look back at the form, maybe at the time you're disappointed, but there were some talented horses that he ran against in those races."

After racing at Saratoga ended for the year, Mott gave Cody's Wish two workouts on the Oklahoma Training Track before shipping him to Churchill Downs, where he had the opportunity to run a one-mile race around one turn, as opposed to two turns for that distance at most other racetracks. The trainer thought—and was ultimately proven 100 percent correct—that one-turn races would be his strength.

There was another advantage to running in Kentucky: Cody could be there, which he told his mother was a critical factor in his namesake's fortunes.

At some point after the races at Saratoga, which the Dormans watched on TV, Cody offered a simple reason why Cody's Wish had not yet won.

"He won't win until I'm there to see him," he told his mother.

That prediction would be tested October 2, 2021, when the horse was entered in a maiden race at Churchill. The Dormans made the hundred-mile trip from Richmond for what was a homecoming of sorts for Kelly, who was born in Louisville and had lived across the river in Clarksville, Indiana, before his family moved back to Columbia when he was one. It had been around thirty years since he had been to the track that sits below the iconic twin spires, and Kelly is sure he was never treated so well.

"I didn't know they had all this stuff cooked up for us," he said. "They told us when we got there to just tell them we're the Dormans and they would take care of everything. I wasn't used to being treated like that, but it was kind of neat. We had a better parking spot than Danny [Mulvihill]

Churchill Charlie was always happy to see Cody and Kylie.
DORMAN FAMILY.

and Mary [Bourne] from Godolphin. We went in and they had a lady right at the gate waiting to lead us around and make sure we were where we needed to be."

The Fox Sports TV cameras were rolling, giving Cody and his family their first taste of the bright lights that would shine on them for the next two years. Several of the jockeys came out to get their picture taken with Cody, a celebrity in the making. Churchill gave Kylie a backpack with coloring books and other swag.

The Dormans were brought to the winner's circle to watch the race. Mike Anderson, Churchill Downs president, came down to meet Cody, something he would repeat on future visits. Kenny McCarthy, who oversees Mott's Churchill division, was only mildly aware of the story behind the horse, but it came into clearer focus when a fan yelled to him, "No pressure!"

"I think it really started to sink in then," McCarthy said. "And of course, the Dormans were there. I remember I was nervous, but in a good way. And I just thought, 'Please, please let this work out.'"

No one had to wait too long to see whether it would, because Cody's Wish was in the first race. For betting purposes, he and a horse named Crump made up a coupled entry—required under Kentucky wagering rules because both horses were owned by Godolphin—that went off as a prohibitive 1–5 favorite. After a slight stumble at the start, Rosario had Cody's Wish closer than in previous races, sitting fifth of seven as they ran out of the chute onto the main track. Moving down the backstretch, Cody's Wish pulled closer without being asked and was just off the lead after a half-mile. A bold move on the turn put him in front at the stretch call, and he ran off to a two-length win.

Cody's prediction—that "his" horse would win if he were there to watch—was proven right, and the celebration was on.

"It was just kind of surreal, shocking," Kelly said. "You had all these emotions running at one time. I think the Churchill people and Danny and the Godolphin people were nervous about everything kind of lining up and falling into place the way it did."

Kelly and Leslie didn't think it could get any better than having a horse named for their son. Now they were posing for an official win photo at Churchill Downs, home of the Kentucky Derby.

Cody didn't show much emotion immediately, but as the day went on, he made it known how he was feeling.

"During the races, you don't really get a whole lot of emotion from him, where so much is going on," Kelly said. "But after the race, especially on the way home, I mean, that kid was still laughing when we got him in bed. Just laughing. He was tickled to death all the way home."

In the Churchill Downs winner's circle, McCarthy asked the Dormans whether he could bring the horse close to Cody. It had been a year since the two had last met at the Thoroughbred Training Center near Keeneland, when Cody was going through his depression, so how either the boy or the horse would react was again very much in question—but not for long.

"Here's a horse that just ran a race," McCarthy said. "I mean, he's a big, strong individual, and he just calmed himself down, and he dropped his nose right there to Cody. It's the most amazing thing. It gives me chills every time I see it. It was like he looked up and was like, 'Hang on a minute. This is our moment. This is Cody and Cody right now. Just give us a moment here.'"

That scene would be repeated over the next two years—on the backstretch, in the paddock, and back in the winner's circle.

Cody's Wish ran two more times as a three-year-old and won both. Jockey Martin Garcia rode him November 6, the same day as the 2021 Breeders' Cup at Del Mar, where Rosario was committed to ride. With the horse entered in the last race, scheduled to go off at 8 p.m., the Dormans opted to watch from home.

Out in California, Team Godolphin was having a banner day, with two of the stable's European stars—Space Blues and Yibir, both trained by Charlie Appleby—winning the Breeders' Cup Mile and the Breeders' Cup Turf, respectively. In the winner's circle after the Yibir race, the Godolphin people from Kentucky were glued to their phones, as interested in a $127,000 allowance race at Churchill as they were in the $4 million Grade 1 they just won.

Regardless of where you watched—Louisville, Richmond, or Del Mar—you could clearly see Cody's Wish was starting to figure it out. Garcia got him involved in the race earlier and he was in the middle of the pack after a quarter-mile, instead of trailing the field. He was already fourth and in the clear at the halfway point, moved to third entering the turn, and put his nose in front at the top of the stretch. From there, Cody's Wish gradually extended his lead, winning by 5¼ lengths and offering no stress for those who bet him at even money and earned a 100 percent return on investment in a minute and a half. Try getting that in the stock market.

The last start of his three-year-old season came November 28, the Sunday of Thanksgiving weekend. Churchill Downs gave the Dormans a suite, allowing them to invite family and friends. "I can't say enough about them," Kelly said. "They treated us like kings every time we've been there."

With Rosario back in the saddle, Cody's Wish was last early on, around ten lengths off the lead, but he started traveling with purpose without being asked. Similar to his previous race, he made a menacing move on the turn and was second at the stretch call. The leader, Ducale, did not surrender without a fight, but Cody's Wish wore him down in the last hundred yards and won by a length.

Cody, a blanket draped on his lap on the forty-five-degree afternoon, was again waiting when the horse returned to the winner's circle. McCarthy, who came to the United States from Ireland at age twenty and has worked for Mott for more than thirty years, and fellow assistant Penny Gardiner, who grew up on a cattle ranch in Colorado and has been working on the racetrack since graduating from high school, joined a happy Dorman clan.

As they tried to get the horse to settle for the photo, Cody had his eyes trained on his friend, who had now won three straight races after three losses to start his career. He was validating the optimism Godolphin and Mott had from the beginning, leading them to believe he could be in line for a productive four-year-old campaign.

Alvarado also had a good year in 2021, winning 110 races and more than $9 million in purses. The day after he rode Cody's Wish in his first race—the one that cost him his job—he won the Grade 1 Jaipur Stakes for Mott on the Belmont Stakes card. At the end of the year, Alvarado rode in four of the Breeders' Cup races, but none of his horses finished in the top four. Through it all, he never forgot about Cody's Wish and took note of his improvement.

"I knew it was going to take him time," he said. "But I wanted to make sure I followed him because I know Bill Mott, that's his way of training horses. They get better, better, and better. So I wanted to make sure even if I couldn't ride him, I kept an eye on him in case I had the opportunity to get back on."

He knew one thing: If he ever did get another shot on Cody's Wish, he would make damn sure he never got taken off again. He couldn't help but wonder whether he would ever get that chance.

11

Saratoga Shocker

AFTER RACING SIX TIMES IN SIX MONTHS AS A THREE-YEAR-OLD, CODY'S Wish went south for the winter, settling in at Bill Mott's winter base at Payson Park in Indiantown, Florida, around ninety minutes northwest of Gulfstream Park. Payson was founded in the 1950s as the St. Lucie Training Center by horse breeder and owner Michael Phipps, a member of one of American racing's royal families; Arthur "Bull" Hancock, under whose direction Claiborne Farm stood the leading sire in the United States every year from 1955 to 1969; and Christopher Chenery, breeder of the legendary Secretariat.

The facility went into decline after Phipps died of a heart attack in 1973, six weeks before Secretariat won the Kentucky Derby on the way to his Triple Crown. In 1980, horsewoman and former *Sports Illustrated* writer Virginia Kraft Payson resurrected and renamed the four-hundred-acre training center and owned it for almost forty years, selling to prominent horse owner Peter Brant in 2019.

Payson Park's twenty-one barns can accommodate five hundred horses, who have the opportunity to train on dirt and turf tracks plus European-style riding trails. It is considered an ideal facility to condition horses, giving trainers such as Mott who are based in New York the chance to escape the Northeast winters. The top three finishers in the 2019 Kentucky Derby (after the disqualification of Maximum Security for causing interference)—Country House, Code of Honor, and Tacitus—all trained at Payson prior to their three-year-old campaigns.

Cody's Wish had almost three months off after the win at Churchill Downs, returning to the work tab at Payson on January 30, 2022. Mott gave him six timed workouts before running him in the Grade 3 Challenger Stakes at Tampa Bay Downs, where he was the 2–1 favorite in a $100,000 race at 1 1/16 miles around two turns.

There is legitimate cause for concern anytime a horse comes in off a 106-day layoff, but not so much with the Hall of Famer Mott calling the shots. In a five-year period starting in 2020, he won 26 percent of the time with horses off layoffs of 90–180 days, putting him in elite status in that category.

There was an X factor, however, that only a few people knew about.

At the Dormans' home in Kentucky, Cody woke up early March 12, and his parents could tell something was bothering him. Thinking it might be a headache or stomachache, they tried to comfort him but weren't successful, so Leslie took out his tablet and asked Cody what was wrong.

"He's not ready," Cody told her. "He's not ready."

"What are you talking about?" Leslie asked.

"My horse," Cody replied.

Kelly reminded him that if the horse were not 100 percent, Mott would not be running him.

"No, he's going to finish second," Cody said.

Undeterred by his son's prediction, Kelly placed a win bet on Cody's Wish through his online wagering account.

With jockey Luis Saez riding him for the first and only time, Cody's Wish broke last—no surprise—and was fifth at the first turn, roughly five lengths off the lead. Saez made a gradual move as they turned for home and was third at the top of the stretch, a half-length behind Scalding, who had taken over the lead from Wolfie's Dynaghost. Running widest of all, Cody's Wish looked like a winner, but he was outdueled by Scalding in the final sixteenth of a mile and had to settle for second.

Just like Cody predicted.

"I learned my lesson that day," Kelly said. "I wasn't messing with him no more. From then on, whatever he said, I wasn't asking any questions."

Mott had thought the horse would have no problem handling longer distances, even though all three wins had come at a mile (eight furlongs) and he had lost at 1 1/16 and 1 1/8 miles, both times around two turns. The loss to Scalding "sort of proved to me at that point that we better shorten him back up to a one-turn race, seven [furlongs] or a mile," the trainer said.

Cody's Wish's next start, the Grade 3 Westchester Stakes at Belmont Park, came May 7, which in 2022 happened to fall on the first Saturday of the month. That was a significant development for Junior Alvarado, who had watched three other jockeys ride the big horse he was taken off after the troubled first race, still wondering whether he would get another shot.

Cody was a sharp handicapper, especially when it came to Cody's Wish. DORMAN FAMILY.

As it turned out, the calendar was his friend.

The Kentucky Derby, arguably the world's most famous horse race, is run at Churchill Downs on the first Saturday in May. In addition to the $5 million Derby, there are as many as eight other stakes races worth up to $1 million each on the card. The jockeys' room that day is like the locker room at the Major League Baseball All-Star Game—athletes at the top of their profession coming to Louisville to participate in the sport's showcase event.

For Alvarado, the bad news was that he didn't have a mount in the Kentucky Derby or any of the undercard races, so he would not be part of one of the most lucrative days of racing. The good news was none of the three jockeys who had ridden Cody's Wish in the last eleven months would be at Belmont that day. Joel Rosario and Luis Saez had Kentucky Derby mounts and Martin Garcia was riding at Oaklawn Park in Arkansas.

That left open the mount on Cody's Wish, and it was up to agent Mike Sellitto to get Alvarado back on.

Alvarado, who rode at Gulfstream in Florida for the winter, stayed behind when most of the top jockeys and horses returned to New York in early April. In his sixteenth year riding in the United States and having experienced notable success—he made the top twenty in earnings eight times from 2012 to 2021—he found himself at a crossroads. He felt he belonged in the top echelon of US jockeys but sensed a decreasing number of others sharing that opinion. He was in a funk.

"My business was slow and I was very disappointed," Alvarado said. "Mentally, I was burned out."

Maybe he would stay in Florida, ostensibly to ride year-round, though he looked at that as more of an exit plan than a relocation.

"I'm telling you, I was like 85 percent out," he said. "I told my wife, 'I'll ride here all year round,' but that was just an excuse. My mind really wasn't in it. I wasn't going to really ride a whole year there because I didn't want it anymore. I was tired. I was disappointed. So many years riding and trying so hard, and things just keep getting taken away from me. I was just disappointed."

He needed a jolt of positive energy, which was supplied when Sellitto called to say he was back on Cody's Wish in the Westchester. When jockeys are replaced on a horse, regardless of the reason, there is no guarantee they will ever regain the mount. When it happens, they are theoretically better prepared, having the experience of the previous race(s) to fall back on and opportunity to make the necessary adjustments.

Alvarado had one mount at Churchill Downs that weekend and made it count, winning the Alysheba Stakes with Olympiad for Mott the day before the Kentucky Derby. First place was worth $303,800 for the connections, and with jockeys typically receiving 10 percent of the earnings, it was a profitable stop.

As Alvarado traveled to New York for the Cody's Wish race, he made a conscious effort to temper his enthusiasm, because he understood why he got the mount back.

"I got the opportunity because everybody was at Churchill that day," he said. "I didn't want to get too excited because I had already ridden him before and got taken off."

Coming off three wins and the loss by a nose in the Challenger Stakes, Cody's Wish was supposed to win. Alvarado knew it, as did the betting public.

"I looked at the PPs [past performances] and the numbers and I thought he should be very competitive in that race," Alvarado said.

All that did was add to the pressure, and when the track came up sloppy, similar to the conditions of the horse's career debut, the jockey felt it.

"It was extremely muddy that day. It was a terrible track," Alvarado said. "So I'm thinking, 'Jesus, I'm going to have this terrible track again when I'm riding this horse. Why?' I just wanted a normal track, and everything to go normal."

Alvarado didn't realize it at the time, but there would never be anything close to "normal" when it came to riding Cody's Wish.

Kelly and Leslie were eager for Cody's prediction, especially after he had nailed it in the previous race. Apparently satisfied the horse was more prepared, Cody told his parents his namesake would win. Knowing he wouldn't be there, Cody sent a video wishing his favorite horse good luck and thanking him for being his friend.

The Westchester drew only five horses, and Cody's Wish went off as the odds-on favorite for the fifth time in eight starts. Something strange happened when the gate opened: Cody's Wish didn't fall back to the rear of the field. In fact, he broke sharply and was second, only one length off the leader, Sound Money, down the backstretch of the one-mile, one-turn race. Alvarado was still sitting chilly when his horse effortlessly gained the advantage going around the turn.

"There goes Cody's Wish now to take the lead from Sound Money," track announcer John Imbriale said. By the time they reached the stretch call, Cody's Wish was well ahead on the way to a five-length victory.

"I remember that race like it was yesterday," Alvarado said nine months later. "He broke out of there very sharp, put me in a good spot, a length behind the horse that was in front. He drew away. He ran an extremely good race that day."

After the race, Alvarado called Sellitto with an urgent request.

"Mike, this horse is very good," the jockey told his agent. "I didn't feel that he loved the track and he still won very impressive with a big number. Listen, there is more underneath there, this is a very nice horse. Let's see what we can do to try to stay on him. I know I got to ride him because nobody was in town. When everybody comes back, I want to try to keep this horse."

The next target was the Metropolitan Handicap, better known as the Met Mile, a prominent race first run in 1891. The one-mile distance, which proved to be Cody's Wish's preference, requires a mix of speed and stamina. The Grade 1 Met Mile is known as a stallion-making race, with horses who win often garnering significant interest when they retire to the breeding shed.

For Mott, winning the Met Mile represented one of the few unchecked boxes in his Hall of Fame career that began in 1973. It looked as if he would have a potent one-two punch in 2022 with Cody's Wish and Speaker's Corner, another Godolphin homebred, who had blossomed as a four-year-old, winning three consecutive graded stakes races. His regular rider? Junior Alvarado.

Also pointing for the Met Mile was Flightline, a lightly raced but supremely talented horse based in California. Undefeated as a three-year-old, Flightline—a son of Tapit, who sired Cody's Wish's dam, Dance Card—was making only the fourth start of his career in the Met Mile. Cody's Wish had already run eight times and Speaker's Corner had nine starts by June of their four-year-old year.

Had both horses run, Alvarado would almost certainly have stayed on Speaker's Corner, but before that scenario materialized, Cody's Wish spiked a fever and missed a workout, prompting Mott to remove him from consideration. The trainer still had Speaker's Corner, a clear second choice in the wagering. To his credit, Alvarado took the fight to the heavy favorite, sending Speaker's Corner to the lead, but Flightline was never far behind and took control on the turn before drawing off by six lengths. Speaker's Corner settled for third.

"We found out the hard way that horse was something else," Alvarado said of Flightline, who won two more races to retire unbeaten and earn Horse of the Year honors for 2022.

By this point, it was clear that Cody's Wish was pretty damn good, too. After three losses to start his career, the big horse had won four of five races, the only blemish the loss at Tampa. Missing the Met Mile presented a logistical challenge in that there were not many opportunities for stakes-caliber horses to run a seven-furlong or mile dirt race at that time of the year. Mott decided to ship Cody's Wish to Churchill Downs for the one-mile Hanshin Stakes on July 4.

"It was either run him at the wrong distance or ship him there," Godolphin's Michael Banahan said.

Alvarado had returned to Gulfstream and, even with the Saratoga meet approaching, planned to stay in south Florida as he contemplated his future. He was sure of one thing: He wanted to stay on Cody's Wish, wherever and whenever he ran.

"I know I'm in Florida now, but what do I do to keep riding this horse, man?" Alvarado asked Sellitto. "This is the beast that they thought it was."

When the race in Kentucky came up, the jockey headed for the airport.

"I went there specifically to ride that horse that day," he said.

When he got to Louisville, Alvarado knew the horse's ability but not the full story. That changed when he met Cody for the first time and was struck by the obvious bond between boy and horse.

"My agent told me the story of why the horse got his name," he said. "I got to the paddock a little late, but one thing I remember is Cody was just staring at the horse. He was looking at the horse like no one else was around. Something was happening there. Looking back, it gives me chills. It's unbelievable."

Once they loaded into the starting gate, Alvarado knew he had his hands full. Cody's Wish had become a bad actor in the gate, and at Churchill that day he actually tried to go *under* the gate, prompting Alvarado to jump off.

"He was extremely upset in the gate that day, like very mean. It was scary. I remember that gate shaking. I'm like, 'No, no, no, no, no,'" Alvarado said, referring to the way a jockey communicates to the starter that it is not OK to open the gate. "I did get off because he tried to go under and he was pulling me under. He was like a beast in the gate. Then I get off and the guy [assistant starter] says, 'Get on the horse.' And I'm like, 'Not until he is on four legs.'"

Once the horse had settled down (or at least become less unmanageable), Alvarado got back in the saddle and prepared for the start.

The Dormans watched the race from the same spot in the winner's circle where they had seen Cody's Wish win twice the previous year. Breaking from the far outside in a field of six as the heavy favorite, Cody's Wish was within two lengths of the lead going down the backstretch. Alvarado made his move on the turn and was in front by the time they straightened for home, but any thoughts of an easy victory were quickly dispelled. Three Technique—a horse once owned by Hall of Fame football coach Bill Parcells—made a menacing move and put his nose in front as it became a two-horse race.

Cody's Wish showed that he relished the idea of an equine street fight, providing a preview of a future tussle. "Emboldened by that challenge, Cody's Wish comes right back," track announcer Travis Stone called it, as Alvarado's mount "battled gamely while clinging to an advantage through the late stages, and held tenaciously," according to the Equibase summary of his win by a neck.

The Dormans were joined by several family members, and, after the winner's circle photo, they were taken to the Directors Room for the traditional champagne toast provided for stakes-winning connections. The Hanshin Stakes trophy was presented to Cody, who had now seen Cody's Wish run in person three times; they were undefeated.

As Godolphin and Mott planned the second half of the horse's four-year-old campaign, they identified the Pat O'Brien Stakes at Del Mar on August 27 as a logical next race. The O'Brien—named for the actor who cofounded the seaside racetrack north of San Diego in 1937 with crooner Bing Crosby—was a seven-furlong, Grade 2 race around one turn, right where Mott wanted Cody's Wish.

On the same day, the Forego Stakes would be run at Saratoga, also at seven furlongs. The Forego was a Grade 1 worth more than twice as much ($600,000 versus $250,000), and the field would include a monster named Jackie's Warrior, who became the first horse to win a Grade 1 race at Saratoga in three consecutive years when he captured the A. G. Vanderbilt Stakes on July 30. The champion male sprinter of 2021, Jackie's Warrior had won the Hopeful Stakes in 2020 and the H. Allen Jerkens Stakes in 2021. He was perfect in five starts at Saratoga and looked unbeatable.

The more Mott thought about it, the more he liked the idea of keeping Cody's Wish home and sending Speaker's Corner to Del Mar. He wanted to give Cody's Wish a chance in a Grade 1, even if it meant taking on Jackie's Warrior. Speaker's Corner, who got his Grade 1 win in the Carter Handicap at Aqueduct in April, had run against arguably the two best horses in the country in his previous two races—Flightline in the Met Mile and Life Is Good in the John A. Nerud Stakes—and Mott wasn't thrilled with the idea of completing that trifecta by putting him in with Jackie's Warrior.

Mott called an audible and entered Speaker's Corner in the Pat O'Brien and Cody's Wish in the Forego. Alvarado was named on Cody's Wish, but he was realistic about his chances.

"You can't beat Jackie's Warrior," he told his agent. "The best-case scenario is we finish second."

Kelly Dorman told a good friend who follows horses and happened to be a huge Jackie's Warrior fan that Cody's Wish was running in the Forego. "I'm not trying to hurt your feelings," his friend told him, "but every other horse in there is running for second."

Kelly, who had read more about the race than any of Cody's Wish's previous nine starts, couldn't argue with him, so he tried to prepare Cody for what looked inevitable.

"I remember telling him that he's got his work cut out for him," Kelly said, but Cody wasn't having it. On the Fox Sports broadcast, the analysts understandably focused the pre-race conversation on Jackie's Warrior, who came into the race with twelve wins in sixteen starts and was less than a month removed from establishing the Saratoga Grade 1 record.

Watching at home, Cody became noticeably restless—not unlike the day of the Challenger Stakes—so Leslie took out his tablet and asked him what was bothering him.

"Will you tell them to shut up?" he said, looking toward the TV and catching his parents by surprise.

"That's not Cody," Leslie said. "That was out of character for him, but he got mad listening to everyone say Jackie's Warrior was going to win."

Cody made a sign in a therapy session wishing Cody's Wish good luck and predicted the horse would win—but only if he saw the sign. His parents sent it to Godolphin, and it was forwarded electronically to Mott, who wasn't about to upset this applecart and showed it to the horse. To those who pay even a moderate amount of attention to horse racing and have a hard time envisioning the old-school Mott showing a racehorse a picture on his cell phone, you're not alone.

When he couldn't be there, Cody made sure his friend knew he was rooting for him. DORMAN FAMILY.

Sellitto relayed all of this information to Alvarado, who nonetheless remained realistic about his chances.

"Mike, if that is all true, then hopefully we'll finish second. It's as simple as that," Alvarado told his agent. "Second or third would be unbelievable. Jackie's Warrior is the best sprinter in the country, maybe the whole world."

Jackie's Warrior went off at 1–9, the lowest odds possible. A $2 win bet on him would return $2.30. Cody's Wish was the second choice but drifted all the way up to 8–1. The bettors agreed with Kelly Dorman's friend: This was a one-horse race.

When it came time to place a bet, Kelly was willing to go against popular opinion—and with his favorite resident handicapper. Not a big bettor by any means, Kelly made a bold-for-him $50 win bet on Cody's Wish.

As the seven horses were loaded into the Saratoga starting gate, Alvarado was concerned about how Cody's Wish would behave, based on the tantrum he threw at Churchill before the Hanshin. The same horse who acted like a puppy when Cody was around had become a handful in the gate on race day.

When Mott gate schooled Cody's Wish in the morning, the horse acted like a professional. In the afternoon, it was a different story, and it was more of the same prior to the Forego, when he moved so forcefully. "I thought he was going to knock that gate down," Godolphin's Banahan said.

In the footage of the Forego, you can see assistant starter Miguel Ramirez holding Cody's Wish's head with both hands in an effort to keep it straight, doing an outstanding job to get the horse standing relatively still when the gate opened.

Pipeline, who had defeated Cody's Wish in two maiden races at Saratoga in 2021, broke first, but Jackie's Warrior didn't have to expend much energy to take the lead in the early stages. Alvarado had Cody's Wish in sixth, but only around five lengths behind.

Jackie's Warrior maintained the advantage into, around, and out of the turn, but he never got any real separation. It was as if Pipeline, ridden by Irad Ortiz Jr., were tethered to him with a taut rope and Rosario, aboard Jackie's Warrior, couldn't shake him. Cody's Wish, meanwhile, was still at the back of the field when Alvarado made a move, splitting horses on the turn and swinging to the far outside as they straightened for home.

"I started picking off horses one by one, and when I got to the quarter pole, there was way more power than I thought I would have at that point," he said. "I had a very good feeling."

By the time Jackie's Warrior finally dispatched Pipeline and put a length between them at the eighth pole, Cody's Wish was in full flight and Alvarado had to convince himself of what was about to happen.

"Am I going to go by this horse? Yes, I'm going to go by this horse."

Cody's Wish took the lead around fifty feet from the finish line and won by 1¼ lengths. Saratoga, known as the Graveyard of Champions, had claimed another victim—forty-nine years after Secretariat lost to Onion in the Whitney Handicap and seven years after Triple Crown champion American Pharoah was upset by Keen Ice in the Travers.

For Team Cody's Wish, it was time to celebrate, both in Saratoga Springs and eight hundred miles away in Richmond, where Cody watched the race holding his sign and the No. 5 green saddlecloth Cody's Wish had worn when he won at Churchill Downs.

Cody's condition might have limited his participation in the bedlam that ensued, but his face emanated pure joy, mixed with a touch of "I told you so."

Back at Saratoga, even the Godolphin folks were caught a little off guard by the shocking upset.

"We were coming in knowing we were running against a champion in Jackie's Warrior," Banahan said. "He's a superstar horse, but our horse deserved a chance at the Grade 1 level. He's progressed each race he's run.

Cody's Wish pulled off a massive upset in the 2022 Forego Stakes at Saratoga.
MATHEA KELLEY.

We felt like there was more in the tank as well. We weren't coming in here thinking we were going to win. We thought if he ran a good second, it would be a good run for him, and if that horse [Jackie's Warrior] stubs his toe or something, we were going to be there to pick up some pieces. We were happy having him in here and taking that chance."

After crossing the finish line first, Alvarado was struck by the thought that maybe there was something special happening and he was involved in a story that transcended horse racing.

"The first thing that comes to my mind when I'm pulling the horse up is like, 'Man, this might actually be true what is happening right now with this horse,'" he said. "I was in disbelief. How did I just beat that horse? I understand in horse racing you have to run the race. But for this horse to run like that and beat Jackie's Warrior? All those things start going through my mind that there had to be something special, something different for us to win this race. I still couldn't believe that just happened."

Among those celebrating the improbable win were friends of Kelly Alvarado's brother, Tommy Short, making their first Saratoga trip without him after he died during the pandemic. COVID-19 wasn't the cause of death, although it might as well have been. Tommy was diagnosed with a blood disease so rare that he needed to go to Cleveland to see a doctor who could treat it. At a time when hospitals were on veritable lockdown, that was not a possibility, and the disease took his life at age fifty-one.

Tommy wasn't there with his sister, brother-in-law, and friends, but they could feel his presence.

"My brother was the one who pushed that horse home," Kelly Alvarado said.

Sellitto encouraged his jockey not to spend too much energy trying to comprehend what might be incomprehensible.

"Things happen," the agent told his jockey. "There are some things that we don't understand and we'll probably never understand. And you just have to believe."

Alvarado was sold. The rest of the racing world would soon follow.

12

Keeneland Reunion

THEY HAD BARELY FINISHED PAINTING THE GODOLPHIN BLUE SILKS ON THE lawn jockey at Saratoga Race Course reserved for the Forego Stakes winner when Bill Mott made the decision to train Cody's Wish in the time leading up to the Breeders' Cup Dirt Mile at Keeneland instead of running him once in between.

Why not? Mott's horse had won the Forego, beating a seemingly invincible favorite, off a fifty-four-day layoff. It would be seventy days to the Breeders' Cup, but what's another two weeks with a Hall of Famer calling the shots?

"There was a brief conversation, but we would have had to change distance and it really wasn't going to work to find him a race in between," Michael Banahan said. "That's why Bill's such a great trainer. It was very similar to the spacing from July 4, when he won the Hanshin, to the Forego."

"I want to run this horse fresh," Mott told Banahan and Dan Pride. "And if it looks like we need something, that's fine, we'll look at that. But I'd rather train him up to the Breeders' Cup."

Mott knew exactly what he was doing. He kept the horse with him at Saratoga, putting in six timed workouts, all on the Oklahoma Training Track, steps from his barn. Mott gave him four half-mile and two five-furlong breezes, all after closing day, when the crowds have left and Saratoga reverts to a peaceful oasis, following two months of a pace so frenetic it can be physically and emotionally draining for equines and humans alike.

"I don't think there was really a race that I wanted to go to," Mott said. "I just felt like he had already proven that he ran pretty well fresh, you know what I mean? Even the Forego. He came into it quite fresh because he won the Hanshin over the Fourth of July weekend."

Mott shipped Cody's Wish to Keeneland a week before the Breeders' Cup Dirt Mile: enough time to settle in and do some jogging and galloping over the 1 1/16-mile oval before trying to win his fourth consecutive race, on one of horse racing's biggest stages.

If there is such a thing as the Thoroughbred capital of the United States, if not the world, it is Lexington, Kentucky. There are almost five hundred horse farms in the area, from storied Claiborne, where Secretariat is buried, to institutions such as Calumet, Taylor Made, WinStar, Spendthrift, Hill 'n' Dale . . . the list goes on and on.

Keeneland was hosting the Breeders' Cup in 2022 for the second time in three years, this one a do-over of sorts after the 2020 edition was run without any fans in the grandstand due to the pandemic, two months after the delayed Kentucky Derby was staged under the same surreal circum-

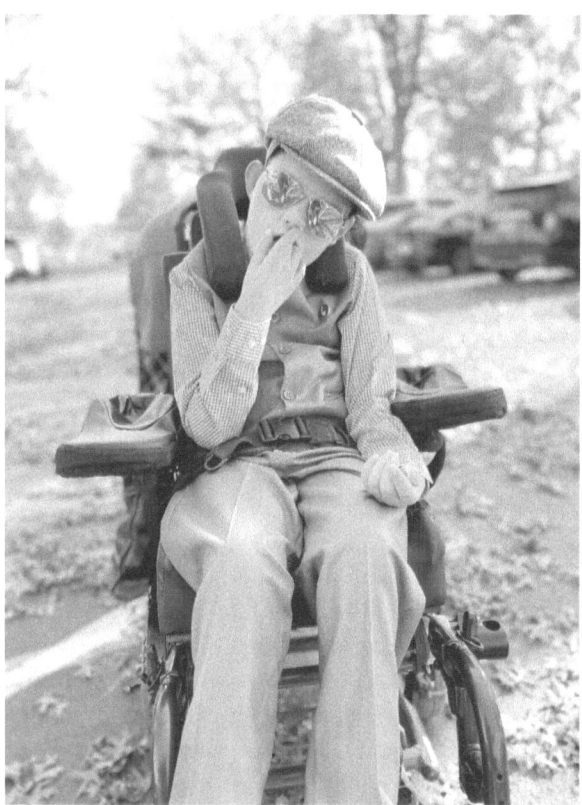

The 2022 Breeders' Cup at Keeneland was a home game for Cody. DORMAN FAMILY.

stances. The 2020 edition was meant to have been a glorious encore after the track had earned almost universal acclaim for its inaugural opportunity to host the world championships in 2015, when Triple Crown champion American Pharoah rebounded from a loss in the Travers with a win in the Breeders' Cup Classic.

The Breeders' Cup was already committed to Del Mar in 2021 but felt it owed Keeneland. No one understood that fact better than Breeders' Cup president and CEO Drew Fleming, a Lexington native and Henry Clay High School graduate who grew up attending the races at the venerable track on Versailles Road.

"I think our teachers knew on Fridays when we showed up in a blazer that we might not be attending class after lunch," Fleming recalled. "You'd often find us at Keeneland on a Friday afternoon."

Fleming's best friend was Gatewood Bell, whose father, Jimmy, served as president and racing manager for Godolphin USA for twenty years and was running the operation when Cody Dorman and Cody's Wish first met.

As a teenager, Fleming got a job cutting grass at Wimbledon Horse Farm on Delong Road, between Overbrook Farm and Juddmonte Farm. He worked for Brian O'Rourke, whose brother, Garrett, runs the hugely successful Juddmonte operation in the United States.

After graduating from Washington and Lee University in Virginia, Fleming came home to attend law school at the University of Kentucky. He was working at a firm that did extensive work in the equine world when he met Breeders' Cup CEO Craig Fravel, who invited him to lunch just before Christmas in 2015.

"In Lexington, there are some fun Christmas lunches," Fleming said, "so I knew when Craig ordered an iced tea there was something serious going on."

A job offer qualifies as serious.

"I want you to stop practicing law and come work for me full-time," Fravel told Fleming. "I can't promise you where this path will go other than I've been in this business for many years and I feel it's important to mentor the next generation."

Fravel made a compelling case for Fleming to make the move.

"He told me he would take me to every meeting and give me a Harvard education in racetrack management and Thoroughbred analysis," said Fleming, who took the job the next day.

Fravel kept his word and brought Fleming into the Breeders' Cup inner circle, including him in meetings, emails, and interactions with board members. When Fravel left to join 1/ST Racing late in 2019, Fleming was tapped to be his successor, a year before the 2020 Breeders' Cup at Keeneland.

Four months into his tenure, Fleming was immersed in an on-the-job crash course in staging horse racing's world championship event when COVID-19 struck. The 2020 Breeders' Cup, like virtually every other activity, was in peril.

The first twenty-three editions of the Breeders' Cup, the brainchild of Kentucky breeder John Gaines, were one-day events, drawing elite horses from North America and Europe to compete for millions of dollars in purse money. They ran for a total of $10 million in the inaugural event at Hollywood Park in 1984. In 2007, the event expanded to eleven races over two days, with $23 million up for grabs. By 2022, when the Breeders' Cup came to Keeneland for the third time, it was a fourteen-race extravaganza—five Friday, nine Saturday—worth $28 million.

In June 2020, Fleming found himself on a conference call with leaders of all the major professional sports leagues, who were asked to update President Donald Trump on the status of their operations. The Breeders' Cup was run as scheduled in November, but with no fans, and while that would have been difficult regardless of the venue, in horse-crazed Kentucky it was especially hard to swallow and left all concerned feeling unfulfilled.

That was a predictable reaction, and one that had been addressed before the races were even run. In September, the Breeders' Cup announced the event would return to Keeneland in 2022, with attendance capped at forty-five thousand, based on the size of the facility.

You could thus conclude that even COVID-19—dirty, rotten, wretched, deadly COVID-19—played a role in this story of the improbable and yet undeniable connection between Cody Dorman and Cody's Wish. The pandemic that turned the world upside down in 2020 resulted in the Breeders' Cup being run a half hour from the Dormans' home in Richmond two years later.

After one of the races Cody's Wish won at Churchill Downs in 2021, the Dormans were talking with Kenny McCarthy, Mott's lead assistant in Kentucky, about the growing media attention. McCarthy was prescient enough to look ahead a full year, to when the Breeders' Cup would be run in the Commonwealth.

"If we get him to the Breeders' Cup, you better be ready," McCarthy said. "You haven't seen anything yet."

As they made the hundred-mile ride home that Sunday after Thanksgiving, Kelly Dorman started thinking about what McCarthy had said, allowing himself to imagine what it would be like for Cody's Wish, the horse suddenly showing star power, to run at Keeneland, in front of their son, who had been proving his championship mettle since he took his first breaths at Baptist Health Hospital in Lexington sixteen years earlier.

"At that moment, it really started sinking in," Kelly said. "Anything's possible. Looking back, all the stars were lining up just perfect. It was one thing right after the other falling into place. That was the first time we really talked about the Breeders' Cup."

After the win in the Forego at Saratoga, the story began to explode. Cody and Cody's Wish were the talk of the racing world, and it started to become apparent that Flightline—an undefeated horse whose effortless brilliance had some comparing him to Secretariat (which was considered blasphemy by those who know better)—might have to share the Breeders' Cup spotlight.

In any other year, a horse with Flightline's résumé would be the unquestionable star of the show, but this was different. And the Dormans could feel it.

"After the Forego, [Cody's story] really got some legs under it," Kelly said. "Maybe I'm looking at it through biased eyes, I don't know. I was enamored by Flightline. I wanted to see Flightline. Super horse and you can't take anything away from him. But I probably saw as much, if not more stuff about Cody's Wish than Flightline."

The Dormans were happy to let others opine on which was the bigger story. They had plenty to do to get ready for the big day.

"It was stressful," Leslie said of the lead-up to the Breeders' Cup, which included making sure they would look their best for the NBC cameras.

Life with Cody meant celebrating what might seem like minor milestones, so when he told his parents he wanted to pick out a new suit, he could have asked for Ralph Lauren himself to measure him and Kelly would have pointed his truck toward Madison Avenue in search of the fashion icon.

"As soon as he figured out we were going to the Breeders' Cup, he said, 'I want a navy pinstriped suit,'" Leslie said.

Don't forget the scally cap.

"I'll tell you something," Kelly said. "That little hat Cody was wearing, that's the only hat we've ever been able to get to fit him just right. His head's so small, usually he wears an infant hat. It was perfect for him. He had that horse racing look to him. It took us seventeen years to find that hat. That was pretty neat."

Cody actually got two suits, one for Breeders' Cup Friday and one for Saturday, and so did his dad. Leslie and Kylie bought new dresses. There

Cody dressed for the occasion when the Breeders' Cup came to town. DORMAN FAMILY.

was plenty of blue in the outfits, in line with the color of the Godolphin silks the jockeys wore.

On Monday of Breeders' Cup Week, the Dormans went to the post-position draw at Rupp Arena, home of the University of Kentucky's storied men's basketball program. Before they saw Cody's Wish draw the No. 7 for the Dirt Mile, they met the connections of Tyler's Tribe, an undefeated horse named for eight-year-old Tyler Juhl, who one week earlier rang the bell at the University of Iowa Stead Family Children's Hospital, signaling that he had completed treatment for leukemia. Owner Tom Lepic named the horse, who was running in the Breeders' Cup Juvenile Turf Sprint, for his grandson.

Neither family knew much about the other's story when they met and struck up a conversation. Leslie immediately hit it off with Tyler's grandmother, Cindy, and the two still keep in touch. The world of inspirational horse racing stories is even smaller than you think.

On Wednesday, Kelly worked a half day; then the family did an interview with a local TV station at Jonabell Farm, home of Darley, Godolphin's US breeding operation. From there, they traveled the few miles to Keeneland so Cody could renew acquaintances with his friend, three days before the biggest race of their lives.

The backstretch of the Breeders' Cup host track can be organized chaos, with horses coming from around the globe to compete in the fourteen world championship races, though the environment is markedly less hectic in the afternoon, when the horses' work is done for the day and the media have moved on to their next tasks. This day at Keeneland was an exception.

Despite efforts to keep it as private an event as possible, word got out that Cody would be coming to visit his namesake, so it was inevitable there would be media. At the top of that list was NBC, which has held the broadcast rights to the Breeders' Cup since its inception in 1984 (other than from 2005 to 2012 when ESPN televised it).

NBC senior vice president and coordinating producer Jack Felling and a crew spent two days in October filming the Dormans—at home; at Gainsborough Farm, where Cody and Cody's Wish first met; and at Keeneland on that year's Make-A-Wish Day. Felling spends most of his time on the Olympics, so he knows an impactful story when he sees one. He typically coordinates the production and assigns others to conduct the interviews, but there was no chance he was giving away this one.

"I keep a great one for myself once in a while," he said. "And for this one, we were in football season so our team was really busy. So, you know what, I said, 'Let me go down there myself,'" though Felling was not convinced how dramatic the interviews would be.

"They're a little reserved and Leslie is a little timid over the phone, so I wasn't really sure what we were getting into," he said. "I knew we'd have a good story and a good shoot, but you don't really know your characters until you're in the room with them. Once I stepped into their home and spent about half an hour with them, I was like, 'This is going to be pretty special.' But you never really know until you get there."

By November 2, three days before the piece was scheduled to air on the Breeders' Cup telecast, Felling was positive they had a great story to show. All it was missing was a climax. Footage of Cody interacting with Cody's Wish would put a bow on it. That couldn't happen, however, without the cooperation of Mott, whose demeanor hints he has neither time nor patience for anything that interferes with the precise regimen required to prepare a racehorse to perform at an optimum level.

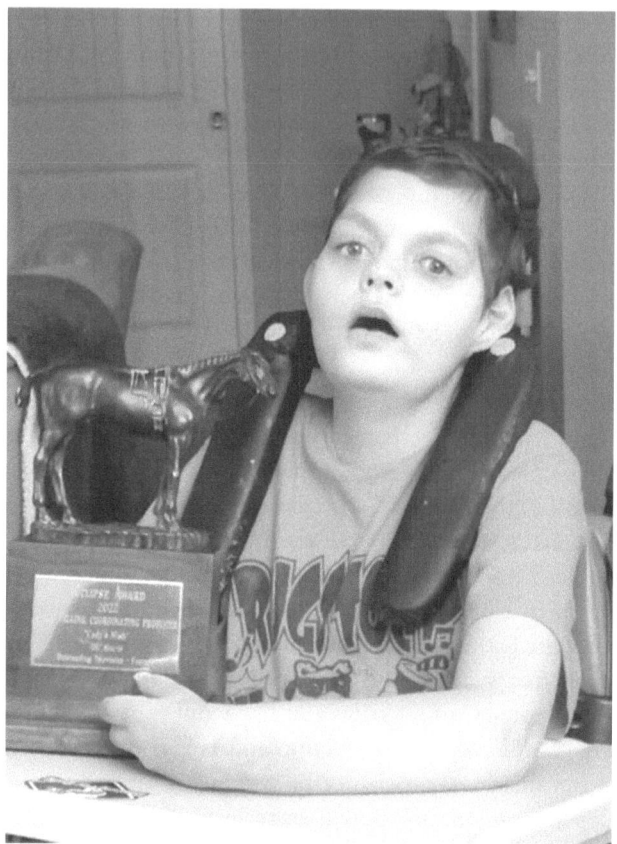

NBC's Jack Felling gave his Eclipse Award trophy to Cody.
DORMAN FAMILY.

Felling recalled that it took "a little convincing" for Mott to allow NBC to film the reunion.

Not so, said the trainer.

"I was all for it. I was fine with it," Mott said, and, after seeing him in similar situations, that is a believable assertion.

One of the myriad sidebars to this improbable story is Mott being coaxed out of his comfort zone. He was sixty-five when Cody first met Cody's Wish and forty-eight years into his training career when Cody's Wish made his debut in June 2021—twenty-three years after becoming the youngest trainer to be inducted into the National Museum of Racing Hall of Fame.

A South Dakota native, Mott has never been a spotlight seeker, preferring to let his horses do the talking. He is all business, viewing distractions as the enemy. And as heartwarming as this story was, a growing level of commotion came with it.

Mott was a willing participant, though it's safe to say having a crowd milling around his barn in advance of a Grade 1 race might not have been his preference. To his credit, though, Mott was keenly aware of the story that was growing beyond the predilections of any one person, even a five-thousand-win Hall of Famer.

That's exactly why he led Cody's Wish out of his Keeneland stall three days before the most important race of the horse's life. Cody was there to see his friend, and Mott was going to do whatever he could to facilitate their latest reunion.

Kelly might have been more worried about disturbing Mott's routine than the trainer himself. After the Forego, when everything started to snowball, Kelly told Godolphin's Dan Pride to always put the horse first.

"You guys are there for a reason," Kelly said. "It's been neat and the story is cool and all that, but under no circumstances let that interfere with why you're there. Just go down there and get the job done."

The team was determined to have Cody see the horse. In addition to the Dormans, there were NBC cameras, other media, and Godolphin staff among the few dozen people standing outside the barn on the Keeneland backstretch when Mott brought out Cody's Wish to see Cody, sitting in the wheelchair where he spent virtually all of his waking moments.

It was eerily quiet and, as he stood next to his son, Kelly was anxious. He had witnessed the almost mystical connection between Cody and the horse, and he wanted so badly for the rest of the world to see it through the NBC lens.

"I was real concerned because I wanted them to catch some of that magic on film," Kelly said. "I didn't know if there were any doubters or naysayers out there. I'm sure there were. That's just the way the world works. But I really wanted them to catch something just to put that to rest if anybody was second-guessing anything."

Previous interactions were limited to the Dormans and the horse's inner circle. On this day there were more people, some armed with cameras, microphones, and notebooks.

Holding the shank, Mott led Cody's Wish toward Cody. The horse stood and looked at the boy for a few minutes, perhaps puzzled by all the commotion. Kelly thought the horse had a look on his face like "Why is everybody here? What's going on?"

Cody's Wish and Cody were no more than six feet apart when the horse walked up and dropped his head in Cody's lap.

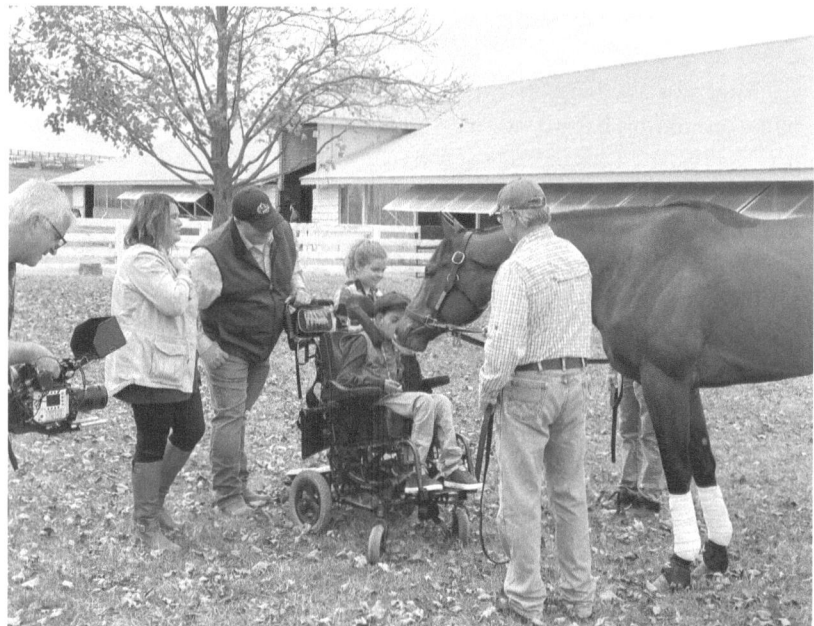

Three days before the Breeders' Cup, there was an emotional reunion on the Keeneland backstretch. DANNY MULVIHILL.

"They've always seemed like they speak their own language," Kelly said. "You can't hear it, but you can feel it. They probably had more hardcore interaction that day than they ever had any other time."

With the cameras rolling, the undeniable proof of the bond between his son and this Thoroughbred athlete was there for the world to see. If anyone were inclined to be skeptical, they could now be told to watch the tape.

The magical moment was not over.

As Cody's Wish raised his head from Cody's lap, he rubbed his muzzle up and down Cody's cheek, acting more like a cuddly cocker spaniel than a strapping steed. You could have heard a flake of hay fall to the ground.

"I don't think I breathed the whole time," Kelly said.

Kelly was crying. Leslie was crying. Kylie was crying. Heck, virtually everyone was crying.

"It was probably one of the most powerful things I've ever experienced," Kelly said. "If you weren't moved by that right there. . . . That hit me like a sledgehammer. I walked off just to kind of get my crap together. I'm on national TV crying like a newborn baby. And I kind of got it back together and I turned around and everybody there was bawling. The only person that wasn't crying was Bill Mott. I looked at Bill and I started to say something to him, but I had no idea what I was going to say. He was just grinning, and he had that look on his face like, 'Don't talk.' When guys are getting ready to break down, you don't say a thing. You just look away. That's what I did."

Mott was taken by the juxtaposition of this picture of equine strength, who he hoped was primed to perform at the highest level, acting so docilely around this severely disabled boy he outweighed by a multiple of fifteen.

"I mean, he's a big, strong horse. He's a lot of horse," Mott said. "There's something about horses, they seem to know when there is a difference in children in situations like that. You might have some untrusting, mean horses, or untrusting, mean people, and they could react differently. But I'd say the better horses are going to react in kind of a positive way."

This latest interaction between Cody and the champion racehorse was especially emotional for his parents, who were struck more than ever by the irony that Cody now had a true friend—albeit one with four legs, though he had never had one with two (his little sister notwithstanding).

"You know, that's one thing that's always bothered Cody, that he didn't have *his* friend," Leslie said. "We told him he had all kinds of friends, but he said, 'I don't have my own friends.' And that was one of the biggest things when he was really depressed. He just wanted a friend. I think he found him."

In upsetting Jackie's Warrior at Saratoga, Cody's Wish had proven he was among the best horses in the country. In seventy-two hours, he would try to become a champion of the world—with his best friend cheering him on.

🐎 13 🐎

"That One's for You, Cody"

THE 2022 BREEDERS' CUP DIRT MILE WAS SATURDAY, NOVEMBER 5, BUT the Dormans weren't about to stay home Friday with day one of the world championship racing taking place a half hour away. Besides, they already had their outfits and it would serve as a dry run for the main event on Saturday.

The Dormans were seated in the Lexington Room, a fourth-floor dining area overlooking the track, at the same table they would have on Saturday. It was a relatively low-key day, but it quickly became apparent they had a celebrity in their midst.

As the family moved about the facility, they were continually stopped by people wishing them luck and asking to take a photo with Cody. The world-class Thoroughbreds might have been the stars of the show, but Cody made a strong case for Best Supporting Actor.

Just how impactful this story of a boy and his equine namesake had become came into focus for Kelly Dorman at the end of the day Friday. They were in line to check out in the merchandise tent when an older woman approached.

"That's Cody, isn't it?"

"Yes, ma'am."

The woman said she attended the Breeders' Cup every year and had traveled a long distance for this one, hoping to see Cody. And there he was.

"She was super sweet," Kelly said. "I thanked her and told her to get her phone, and we could take a picture of her with Cody."

The woman stood next to Cody and tried to smile through her tears, deeply touched by the encounter.

The Dormans were ready for Breeders' Cup Friday at Keeneland. DORMAN FAMILY.

"I could have dropped a gold bar in her lap and it wouldn't have meant as much to her," Kelly said. "I will never forget that moment. It was really neat."

They were up early in Richmond on Breeders' Cup Saturday. The girls put on their dresses, Leslie in Godolphin blue and Kylie in navy. Cody was anxious to wear his navy pinstripe pants and vest, with matching scally cap and horse racing bow tie, a gift sent by a fan in England. Kelly stuck to the dress code, donning a steel-blue suit and matching tie. If they were going to end up in a winner's circle photo, they would be dressed for it.

After arriving at Keeneland, it didn't take long for the Cody love to resume. "There's Cody!" one woman yelled as they waited to go through security. Another woman in the group smiled as she watched the exchange. It was Barbara Banke, owner of Stonestreet Farm, founded by her late husband, Jess Stonestreet Jackson Jr., who had campaigned two-time Horse of the Year Curlin, the sire of Cody's Wish.

Curlin stands at Hill 'n' Dale at Xalapa, a breathtaking farm in Paris, Kentucky, around twenty-four miles northeast of Lexington. Kelly mentioned to Banke they had been hoping to visit Curlin. She extended an open invitation, handing him a Jackson Family Wines business card.

"Anytime you want to take Cody to see Curlin," said Banke, whose husband had started Kendall-Jackson Wine in 1982, "you contact me directly and I'll make sure everything is taken care of."

"This day is off to a great start," Kelly thought.

The Dirt Mile was the third Breeders' Cup race that day, scheduled for 1:12 p.m. All three times they had watched Cody's Wish run in person, the Dormans went to the paddock to see him before the race. All three times, the horse won, so they weren't about to go off script. At Keeneland, they were escorted by David Dean, one of the hundreds of green-jacketed

Cody enjoyed a quiet moment at Keeneland, one of America's premier racetracks, amid the hubbub of the Breeders' Cup. DORMAN FAMILY.

staff who make visiting the track such a pleasant experience. (Dean, who remained close to the Dormans, died in 2025.)

To get to the racetrack, the horses circle the paddock and follow a path through a tunnel that runs under the grandstand. The walk leading to the tunnel is always lined with fans; on Breeders' Cup Day, they were five deep. The Dormans followed behind the line of nine horses, past veteran Keeneland Green Jackets Jim Navolio and Kevin O'Keeffe, and headed for the winner's circle to watch the race—another undefeated routine.

It had been seventy days since Cody's Wish shocked the racing world at Saratoga, plenty of time for the story of the connection between boy and horse to gain traction, especially within the racing world and definitely in Kentucky. Kelly and Leslie knew of their son's burgeoning celebrity but were still unprepared for that walk.

"Go, Cody."

"Good luck, Cody."

"CODY!"

For many, Cody Dorman and Cody's Wish now comprised a single entity—part boy, part horse, all magic.

As Kelly pushed Cody through that tunnel, he was taken back thirty-five years to his high school days, running onto the football field.

"I thought I'd never have a feeling like that again," he said. "I had all I could do to hold it together. The more we walked, the louder it got."

Kelly only had to wait another ten minutes to experience an adrenaline rush that dwarfed even that.

The Dormans and members of Team Godolphin set up shop in the trackside winner's circle, roughly an eighth of a mile from the finish line. The horses would come by them as they completed their warm-up and went to the starting gate, so they made sure Cody was positioned right on the rail, in plain view of the track.

"I'm walking to the gate, [and] there's this moment where Cody is right there," Junior Alvarado said. "My horse is very happy, he's on his toes, and then all of a sudden he stopped for a second, turned his head, and looked to the outside, where Cody was sitting. My heart started beating a hundred miles an hour again."

More drama would come in the starting gate and on the track. And the network charged with telling the story had to deal with some off-screen angst before the broadcast even got started.

The Dirt Mile was the first Breeders' Cup race televised by NBC that day, broadcast on the USA Network, which it owns. The show was slated to start at 1 p.m., not leaving much time for pre-race analysis. The window got even smaller when a Premier League soccer game on USA—Manchester City versus Fulham—ran long.

The piece on Cody and Cody's Wish that Jack Felling had produced was in the can and ready to go. It was just under six minutes. The clock ticked and everyone at NBC who had viewed the segment knew how compelling it was. If they couldn't fit it in before the race, it might go unwatched, with six Breeders' Cup races to follow, each with its own subplot.

In rehearsal that day, Lindsay Schanzer, award-winning producer of NBC's Breeders' Cup broadcast, made sure the on-air talent watched the piece. Good idea.

"She knew how powerful and how impactful it was," said Ahmed Fareed, who anchored the broadcast. "I was sitting next to [analyst] Randy Moss and he was a little bit reluctant to watch because he knew how emotional he would get."

Moss watched in rehearsal and told Fareed, "I'm not going to be watching that again when we're on the air. I'm going to take my earpieces out and look away. I'm going to be a mess if I watch that moments before I have to talk on TV."

Thankfully, Erling Haaland scored on a penalty kick in stoppage time to give Manchester City a 2–1 win. Schanzer made it clear that if they had time for nothing else prior to the race, including the post parade showing the horses entering the track, the Cody piece would run.

The show came on the air and, rather than an extended intro to set up the day of championship racing, Fareed gave a quick welcome and went right to the segment, narrated by Tom Hammond, who had retired from full-time work in 2018 after broadcasting thirteen NBC Olympics, the NFL, the NBA, and more than two dozen Breeders' Cups for NBC.

"Jack [Felling] called me out of retirement for this one," said Hammond, who was aware of the story but not fully prepared to be as moved as he was when he first read the script. "I didn't know the depth of the connection between Cody and the colt. That's when I knew it was the feature of a lifetime. It touched me as much as any piece ever has in more than fifty years of broadcasting."

The NBC piece on Cody concluded as post time neared and the horses approached the starting gate. Sitting atop Cody's Wish, Junior Alvarado felt the weight of the horse racing world on his shoulders. The jockey knew the magnitude of the race could not be quantified, even in a sport driven by wagering. He was fully aware that if the clock somehow struck midnight on this Cinderella story, he would be cast as Lady Tremaine.

"I will be the villain of the story," he told his wife leading up to the race. "If I don't win this race, they have the villain—that would be me. I destroy the whole thing. I don't even know if I feel comfortable with all this. It was Flightline [in the Breeders' Cup Classic] and it was the story of Cody's Wish. Those were the two big things happening at Breeders' Cup. Even if I do everything perfect and I don't win, I will feel like I'm the one that ruined this."

Cody's Wish's propensity to act up in the gate was another cause for concern, especially when he drew post seven. They load two horses at a time at Keeneland. In a nine-horse field, the No. 1 and No. 5 horses go in first, then the No. 2 and No. 7. There would still be five horses left to load once Alvarado and Cody's Wish were locked into the two-foot-wide enclosure.

Alvarado discussed his concerns with trainer Bill Mott when the post positions were drawn.

"Bill, this horse is going to be in there for a long time," he told him. The trainer said he had schooled Cody's Wish in the gate in the morning and the horse was a perfect gentleman, mirroring how he acted when around Cody.

The reassurance only slightly assuaged Alvarado's concerns, who had lived through the horse's obstreperousness more than once, including in his most recent start at Saratoga.

Alvarado wasn't the only human in the starting gate under the gun. The assistant starter assigned to Cody's Wish was Caleb Hays, considered one of the best in Kentucky, who in 2025 was named head starter at Churchill Downs and Turfway Park.

A lifelong Kentuckian, Hays was born into racing. His late father, Dan, was a trainer and his mother, Carol, worked as a groom and ponied horses on the track. One brother, Chris Herrell, was a jockey, and another, John Hays, also worked on the gate crew. Caleb started at River Downs (now Belterra Park) in Ohio when he was eighteen and was a fifteen-year veteran by the time he led in Cody's Wish at the 2022 Breeders' Cup.

Hays found out three minutes before the Dirt Mile that he would have Cody's Wish, and, considering the horse's reputation, it was as if head starter Jeff Powell had unknowingly played a bad joke on him.

In the race immediately before the Dirt Mile, the Breeders' Cup Turf Sprint, Golden Pal was one of the heaviest favorites of the weekend, coming in with eight wins in twelve starts. He also had a history of acting up in the gate, but Hays had handled him in a stakes race at Keeneland a month earlier without incident and Golden Pal won easily. Still, Hays was on his toes on Breeders' Cup Saturday, especially with a $1 million purse at stake.

Getting off to a clean start is important in any horse race, but it is absolutely critical in a race like the Turf Sprint, a 5½-furlong dash that is over in roughly a minute, making the margin of error infinitesimal. After the last of fourteen horses was loaded, they were ready for a start, waiting for Powell to send them on their way. So far, so good.

Then, disaster.

Golden Pal jerked his head a split second before the gate opened and hopped at the start, breaking dead last and effectively eliminating his chances of winning. Jockey Irad Ortiz Jr. hustled him to within two lengths of the lead heading into the turn, but he never got any closer and finished tenth. If you watch the head-on version of the replay, you can see Hays hang his head after the horses leave the gate.

"I was ready for him and he got me at the last second," Hays said. "It cost him the race and I was beating myself up badly over that one. You feel terrible because you know the money that's on the line and every camera in the country is pointing right at you. It's like going into a boxing match and getting pummeled."

Hays didn't have much time to lick his wounds, especially with seven more Breeders' Cup races that day and the $1 million Dirt Mile up next. When he got the Cody's Wish assignment, Hays knew he would be right back in the spotlight, with a chance for immediate redemption—or another debacle. Like Kelly Dorman, he compared it to football.

"It's like you're the quarterback and right after you throw an interception, they call another pass play," he said.

In the same way that coaches scout opponents, the assistant starters try to do their homework on horses they will handle. Hays quickly spoke with his good friend Anthony Mathias, who had been in the gate with Cody's Wish at Churchill Downs when the horse tried to go under it.

At Keeneland, Mathias, who was assigned to Gunite in the Dirt Mile, warned Hays what he was getting into. "He told me this horse is an absolute bear in there," Hays said.

Powell decided Cody's Wish would be loaded with the front doors of the gate open, a tactic sometimes used with rambunctious horses. Hays walked backward as he guided him in and then hopped up onto the small ledge assistant starters stand on, to the left of the horse. The gate now closed, Alvarado didn't like the way his horse was standing and asked Hays to reposition him, to whatever degree any human can move an eleven-hundred-pound equine.

The jockeys and assistant starters work as a team, so Hays wanted to make sure Alvarado was positive that was what he wanted. "If I'm pushing him and he's not in the mood to be touched and messed with, he's getting more and more aggravated," Hays said. "Do we want to move him and aggravate him, or do we leave him alone and take your chances that maybe he doesn't get the cleanest break?"

After a brief exchange, Hays opted to slightly reposition Cody's Wish, knowing that if the horse revolted, there would conceivably still be enough time to get him settled down. Especially after the Golden Pal mishap, he wanted to ensure that he gave Cody's Wish every opportunity to have a clean break. He somehow got him standing almost still—a herculean feat.

In the thirty seconds it took to load the rest of the field, Alvarado grabbed Cody's Wish's mane with one hand, the reins with the other. Then he prayed.

"Please, God, do not let him stumble. Help me after that, but please don't let him stumble out of the gate. . . . I'm not going to fall. I'm not going to fall."

That was the jockey's immediate goal for the start of the most important race of his life, and the fighting spirit with which Cody Dorman had lived every minute of his.

Powell pushed the button to open the gate, and Alvarado's prayers were answered. The horse did not stumble or fall, but he still broke second last. Alvarado took him to the inside in an effort to save ground on the first turn, knowing he would likely not have that luxury when they entered the stretch.

Pipeline—who had softened up Jackie's Warrior in the Forego at Saratoga—set an honest pace, going a half-mile in 45.71 seconds. That was good news for Alvarado and Cody's Wish, though they were still last at the halfway point and it looked as if Kelly and Leslie would have to explain to their son why they would need to vacate the winner's circle—a concept unknown to him at that point.

Heading into the far turn, Alvarado nudged Cody's Wish and he responded, starting to pick off horses.

"You can see right there, right there. He jumped into the bridle," Alvarado said one morning at Gulfstream Park, watching the replay on an iPad. "I told the guy outside me, Francisco [Arrieta, jockey on Senor Buscador], 'Let me out, let me out.' And he did let me out." (In 2024, Alvarado rode Senor Buscador to a win in the $20 million Saudi Cup, earning more than $1 million in his biggest payday ever.)

Alvarado swung wide on the turn, with Cyberknife (a talented three-year-old who ran in the Kentucky Derby) and Gunite battling closer to the rail. When it became a two-horse battle with an eighth-mile to go, Al-

Junior Alvarado and Cody's Wish outdueled Cyberknife in the stretch in the 2022 Breeders' Cup Dirt Mile. BOBBY SHIFLET/FRAMES ON MAIN GALLERY.

varado moved Cody's Wish closer to Cyberknife, knowing his horse loved a fight. Cody's Wish finally put his nose in front with around ten yards left and hit the finish line first, winning by a head.

"Oh, the wish has come true. That one's for you, Cody," NBC announcer Larry Collmus shouted on the broadcast.

Having watched the segment on Cody and Cody's Wish that morning, Collmus was prepared for an emotional call, but that line was unscripted.

"That one was off the cuff," he said. "Normally in these big races you think of different lines, but in this case it was just what came out."

When it was Fareed's turn to speak, the NBC anchor fought to hold it together.

"Oh, my gosh," he said, his voice trembling. "It's a story made for Hollywood. It was written right here in Lexington, Kentucky."

Fareed, who has covered several Olympics in more than twenty years of broadcasting, had jotted down that line as the horses came down the stretch. He's glad he did, because the emotion of the moment made spontaneity a struggle.

"I think it was definitely the first time in my broadcasting career that I was noticeably emotional on the air," he said. "I had a hard time not being even more emotional. I'm trying not to start bawling on the set. So I tried to say as few words as possible."

Cody was the center of attention in the winner's circle after the Dirt Mile, getting a thumbs-up from assistant trainer Neil Poznansky. GODOLPHIN.

His partners, Moss and Hall of Fame jockey Jerry Bailey, fared only marginally better. To their credit, they balanced the need to provide analysis with letting the moment breathe as the images told the story.

In the winner's circle, there were tears of joy—the kind you feel when you want something so badly and you see it unfold right before your eyes—shed by Cody's parents, sister, Godolphin staffers, and Cody himself. Countless others in the stands at Keeneland and watching on TV had similar reactions.

Asked how he was feeling at that time, Cody said, "I was very nervous, but I knew he would win. It was so magical, especially seeing so many happy people. I was so excited and happy. I was just so proud for Cody's Wish. He saved my life, without a doubt. It's a blessing. I want to thank God for letting me have this experience."

As Alvarado jogged Cody's Wish back to the winner's circle, the jockey had a lot to process. In his sixteenth year of riding in the United States, this was his first Breeders' Cup win, but that was not his focus. Instead, he was thinking about four children—the one in the wheelchair waiting in the winner's circle and his own three. Feeling relieved, he returned to prayer, this time in thanksgiving.

"Thank You, God, for letting me be part of this," he said.

Later, he put the win in perspective.

"I have three kids," the jockey said. "I have a very good idea of what this probably meant for Cody and for the family. I can't even describe the excitement that I had for them. I never felt so happy for somebody else in my life until that race. I think God helped me deliver this. This kid needed a break, needed something to look forward to, something to be happy for."

When the Dormans finally got back to their table in the Lexington Room after a celebratory toast in the Keeneland clubhouse, Kelly got a call from a friend, who said he was with someone who wanted to come by and meet Cody. Ten minutes later, Kentucky governor Andy Beshear was at their table, offering his congratulations and extending an invitation to visit the state capitol in Frankfort. He said he would make Cody acting governor for fifteen seconds.

What a day.

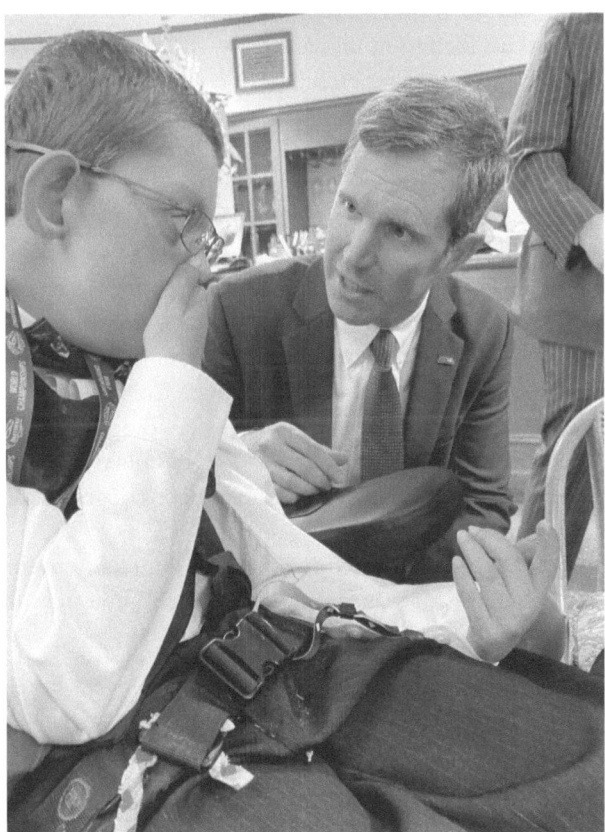

Kentucky governor Andy Beshear stopped by to congratulate Cody on the big win. DORMAN FAMILY.

As they tried to fully comprehend what just happened, Kelly recalled another day at Keeneland with Leslie, eighteen years prior. On April 9, 2004—Good Friday—the newlyweds went out for a day at the races. The Keeneland fans generally dress better than your average racetrack crowd, so Kelly put on his best khakis, button-down shirt, and boots.

"I didn't own a sport coat or tie, so I went with the George Strait look," he said, invoking the country music icon.

It was the usual packed house, and they parked on the grass between the far turn and the backstretch and took the long walk to the frontside to buy general admission tickets. Between the size of the crowd and how well turned out they looked in their suits and dresses, Kelly felt a bit out of place. You can take the guy out of Columbia, but you can't take Columbia out of the guy.

After a few races, he asked Leslie whether she might want to leave and she agreed. As they walked back to the car, a race went off and they stopped on the rail for a bird's-eye view of the horses running by. They spotted a tree and decided to sit under it for a while. No crowd, no betting, no cell phones . . . just enjoying each other's company and, every half hour, watching majestic Thoroughbreds streak by.

Fast forward to November 5, 2022, and here Kelly and Leslie were, on the fourth floor of this historic racetrack, dressed to the nines, legendary trainers Bob Baffert and D. Wayne Lukas a few tables away. Kelly started laughing, and Leslie wondered what was so funny.

"You remember that day we came here right after we were married?" he asked her. "Look at us now."

They were a few hundred yards—and a lifetime—away from that tree.

In preparing for calling the Breeders' Cup, Collmus uses homemade flash cards to memorize the horses in each race, coloring the jockey silks on one side and writing the name of the horse and notes on the other. He sent Cody the card for Cody's Wish, with a note congratulating him on his horse's big win.

Collmus went to his mailbox one day and found an envelope with a Kentucky return address. It was a handwritten thank-you note from Cody that read:

Larry, Thank You!
Love,
Cody Dorman
Cody's Wish

"I could have gotten a million-dollar check in the mail and if I had to choose between that and Cody's note, you could throw the check away," Collmus said.

14

Unfinished Business

As the euphoria from the Breeders' Cup settled in, with the holidays approaching, Kelly and Leslie Dorman found themselves reflecting on the journey their son and this horse had traveled, bringing them and so many others along for a magical ride.

As much as they felt like they were living in a fairy tale, they had video and photographic evidence that it was indeed real, not to mention the living proof they saw every day in a new-lease-on-life Cody.

From the time Cody was born, through more than forty operations and hundreds of other medical issues that followed, his parents came to realize they had no choice but to modify their hopes and dreams for their son. Their long-term goal was whittled to this: Have him survive—and thrive, whatever that might look like for someone faced with a lifetime of challenges.

Having a champion racehorse named for him and ending up on national TV? That was not on the Dorman family bingo card.

"Things like this don't happen to our kids," Leslie said. "To see this is very unusual. I think it speaks volumes for what can happen to anybody."

Still, Kelly and Leslie were always careful to make sure there was room in Cody's spotlight for his sister.

"We work hard to keep things as normal for her as possible," Leslie said. "I think she does get jealous at times. If I see it, I always try to go have a word."

Kelly sometimes sensed during TV interviews that Kylie wanted to talk, so he would try to include her in the conversation. As it turns out, when the camera is on, Kylie's shy streak shines through—although there would be a day when she would find herself in the spotlight on one of horse racing's biggest nights.

Leslie and Cody outside the First Turn Club at Churchill Downs on Kentucky Derby Day 2023. DORMAN FAMILY.

If she ever resented the amount of attention Cody was suddenly receiving, she didn't show it.

"I thought it was really cool," Kylie said about her brother's celebrity status. "I liked being part of it."

As they tried to digest how much Cody's Wish had changed their son's life, Leslie and Kelly gained an even deeper appreciation for those who played a role, before and after Danny Mulvihill brought the foal out of his stall at Gainsborough Farm in 2018: the doctors, especially Dr. Hopkin, the geneticist, and Dr. Thomas, the neurologist; the teachers and therapists; their family and friends; Godolphin and Make-A-Wish.

What Leslie and Kelly could probably never fully comprehend is how impacted those people were by the courageous, relentless resilience of Cody and his family.

Rick Gregory worked with Kelly at Toyota, and their mutual love of bass fishing sparked a friendship. After Cody was born, Kelly called him with the good news, tempering it with "We had a little trouble." It didn't take long for Rick to figure out "a little trouble" was akin to calling the *Titanic* a minor marine mishap.

Rick and his wife, Deata, had experience with Cincinnati Children's, having taken their daughter there for treatment for type 1 diabetes, and he was happy to recommend the hospital to the Dormans. With an eyewitness view of what life with Cody was like for Kelly and Leslie, Gregory saw a sense of resilience he did not think possible.

"I want to tell you, they are pillars of stone," he said. "I have never heard either one of them get down in the dumps. I promise you, never. You never see them without a smile on their face, without something good to say. I don't know how they do it. I can tell you they are just superhuman."

Spending a lot of time with the Dormans, Gregory had a chance to see Cody as more than a boy in a wheelchair, ravaged by a horrific disease. Once Cody got his communication tablet, Leslie's theory about his having a wealth of knowledge trapped inside his debilitated body was confirmed, but Gregory could sense that intelligence well before then.

"He knows everything that is going on around him," he said. "He recognizes things that others don't realize and he wants to be part of everything. He's just a normal kid, except he has that disease. And he's the toughest kid ever on the planet Earth."

Like Kelly, Robbie Harmon is from Columbia and an avid fisherman. He was at the Bassmaster Classic in 2019 when the event recognized Cody and many of the competitors wore the "Casting for Cody" shirts. Harmon was impressed by the likes of fishing legends Kevin Van Dam and Mark Zona acknowledging Cody's toughness.

Harmon shared the story with his son, Jay, who started communicating with Cody through videos and messages. Even as a twelve-year-old, Jay could appreciate how challenging life was for Cody, and he and his dad were anxious to do anything to brighten it.

Cody sent Jay a "Casting for Cody" shirt, and Jay, a baseball player who loves the game, modified it to "Catching for Cody." Sports in general, and baseball in particular, seemed like logical common ground for the two boys.

Robbie and Jay were aware of Cody's mental health struggles during the pandemic and vowed to find a way to connect with him once normal life returned. In summer 2022, Jay played in an all-star game in Louisville for the Etown Shock travel team. At bat in the fourth inning, he turned on an inside fastball and made solid contact. When the ball landed on the other side of the fence, Jay had his first career home run.

His grandfather tracked down the ball and gave it to Jay for a keepsake, but he had other ideas.

Robbie and Jay made a video and sent it to Cody, Jay telling him to check his mailbox for a gift coming his way. It was the home run ball.

"I feel very lucky, very blessed to be playing sports," Jay said. "That's the least I could do for him with all he's gone through."

Jay met Cody in person at a college football game that fall. Seeing their healthy son, the youngest of their three children, interact with Cody, who was in a wheelchair, affected Robbie and Tobie Harmon.

"It's emotional because of the connections that are made," Harmon said. "Sports are sports. One of these days the balls will go flat and the bats will break. Those connections and that love that we have for one another through those sports is the important stuff. It really made my wife and I look in the mirror. We're pretty lucky. We've got two girls in college that can grow and flourish. We've got Jay and he's a teenage boy with all the good, bad, and indifferent, but, man, that's a blessing. Kelly and Leslie and Kylie need to know that they're inspirations to us, because they don't miss a beat. They've got a normal teenage boy just like we do, and they roll with it. It looks a little different, but the love and connections that they share with the world has been pretty impactful."

Cody missed out on plenty of teenage activities, but he didn't want the junior prom to be one of them and he caught his parents off guard when he scored a date.

The prom?

Yes—and with an older woman.

Occupational therapist Janna Lopez started working with Cody in the fall of 2021. She spent a lot of time trying to help him get more use out of his hands, using his love of fishing as a motivator.

Kelly took an old fishing rod and cut it down to fit Cody. He tied some fishing line to it with a magnet on the end of the line and then took several plastic fishing baits and inserted nails into them so the magnet would grab them and Cody could "fish" them out of a bucket.

Kelly took an old tackle box and cleaned it up for Cody to put his baits in. Using a label maker, he covered it with inspirational and funny quotes. Cody loved that tackle box and wasn't amused when his sister got too close to it.

Lopez was responsible for Cody fulfilling his desire to send handwritten notes, such as the thank-you that NBC announcer Larry Collmus received after the 2022 Breeders' Cup.

Janna Lopez was Cody's prom date, and they traveled in style, in a 1955 Chevy Bel Air. DORMAN FAMILY.

During one of their sessions in spring 2023, Cody used his tablet to ask Lopez a question: "Will you go to the prom with me?" Lopez looked at Leslie, who had no idea that was coming. They asked Cody whether he was serious—he most certainly was—and Lopez's answer was a resounding "Yes," even before she cleared it with her husband, Luis. There was a point at which Cody's high school was not going to allow him to bring a thirty-two-year-old date, but common sense scored a victory and the school relented.

Early in the morning of April 29, Cody's Wish had a half-mile workout at Churchill Downs in preparation for the first start of his five-year-old campaign. That night, Cody and Lopez went to the Madison Central High School prom—driven in a classic 1955 Chevy Bel Air by Brad Myers, the close friend who had attended Cody's Make-A-Wish trip to Bass Pro Shops headquarters. The car belonged to Myers's father-in-law, Kermit Hall, who drove it two and a half hours from Beaver, Kentucky. They were escorted to the prom by a parade of classic cars driven by members of the Old School Customs Car Club in Richmond.

Cody stole the show. Again.

One week later, it was time for his namesake to get back on track and start validating Godolphin's decision to run him as a five-year-old rather than retire him to stallion duty, which wouldn't have been surprising considering how much value a horse with his pedigree and achievements has in the breeding shed. Yet even after a year in which Cody's Wish won four of five starts and a Breeders' Cup race, there was an odd sense of unfinished business. Or maybe it was simply a desire to see what he and Cody could do for an encore.

As trainer Bill Mott mapped out a 2023 campaign, he targeted the Met Mile at Belmont, the race Cody's Wish was forced to miss the year before. Mott wanted to win it, and so did the people at Godolphin, who have a deep respect for the history of the sport and an appreciation for the Met Mile's status as one of America's iconic races.

"I think winning a Met Mile was on our mind, knowing he was very effective at a mile," Mott said in typically understated fashion. "Ultimately, I think that was the primary goal for the entire year."

Mott gave the horse seven workouts at Payson Park before shipping him in late April to Kenny McCarthy at Churchill Downs. The comeback race for Cody's Wish would be the Churchill Downs Stakes, on the Kentucky Derby undercard on May 6. Mott is the last person who would consider the dramatic effect of running on Derby Day, but the folks at NBC were ecstatic to have this subplot dropped into their first-Saturday-in-May broadcast lap.

The day before the race, Faith Hacker of Make-A-Wish arranged for Leslie and Kylie to be properly pampered, from picking out new dresses, hats, and jewelry to being treated to a gamut of spa treatments. The Dorman girls would fit right in with the Kentucky Derby crowd, which placed a premium on sartorial splendor.

The Dormans arrived at 11 a.m. and were greeted by track mascot Churchill Charlie, who had befriended Cody and Kylie on their previous visits. They made their way to a table in the newly opened First Turn Club dining area, their arrangements, as always, taken care of by Godolphin.

It had been six months since Cody's Wish raced, but it was clear fans had not forgotten the story:

"You have a beautiful family."

On the way to the paddock for the 2023 Churchill Downs Stakes, Cody's Wish stopped for a quick visit. PAUL HALLORAN.

"Good luck today."

"I'm looking forward to the tenth race [Churchill Downs Stakes] more than the Derby."

An hour before post time, the Dormans were taken to a trackside area adjacent to the winner's circle, with Cody stationed on the rail where Cody's Wish would walk by on his way to the paddock to be saddled. As McCarthy approached with the horse, he stopped in front of Cody for another one of those wordless exchanges that grabbed at the hearts of those looking on. Kylie was brought to tears by the sight of her big brother and his best friend just doing what they did.

Unconcerned about the long layoff, bettors sent Cody's Wish off as an odds-on favorite. With 150,335 fans watching from beneath the twin spires and more than fourteen million on TV, Cody's Wish was last early on and seventh after a half-mile, leaving plenty of work to do. By the time the field turned for home, Junior Alvarado and Cody's Wish loomed on the outside. They took the lead with a furlong left and cruised to a 4¾-length win.

If there were any doubts about the horse being as good—or even better—as a five-year-old, they were erased in the eighty-one seconds it took for him to travel the seven furlongs of the Churchill Downs Stakes.

Cody's Wish won for the eighth time in twelve starts and was now a perfect 5-for-5 with Cody watching live. Included among the eight horses he beat that day was his half brother, Endorsed, also out of Dance Card.

"I don't even know how to describe how much better he got today," Alvarado said after the race. "What I felt today is what you want to feel when you ride horses in big races, to feel the whole machine underneath you. He was just a lovely animal to ride. He was there with me every step of the way. When I asked him, he didn't hold anything back, he just went by those horses."

Among those gathered in the Directors Room for the champagne toast were Governor Andy Beshear and Kate Chenery Tweedy, daughter of Secretariat's owner, Penny Chenery, there to celebrate the fiftieth anniversary of Secretariat's Kentucky Derby triumph.

Tweedy told Kelly and Leslie how touched she was by the story of Cody and Cody's Wish. It was a brief and yet poignant exchange between the child of one horse racing icon and the parents of another.

In the thirty-five days between the Churchill Downs Stakes and the Met Mile, Mott gave Cody's Wish three timed workouts on the Oklahoma Training Track at Saratoga. He was extra sharp in all three, registering the two fastest four-furlong works and the quickest five-furlong breeze of his career, which included sixty-six workouts combined at those two distances. He did this on a track where the workout times are typically slower than most tracks, due to a deeper racing surface.

Who says horses can't talk? The big horse had announced his readiness for the Met Mile, first run in 1891 at Morris Park in the Bronx, a racetrack that hosted the Belmont Stakes from 1890 to 1904.

The original plan was for the entire family to make their first trip to New York, but Cody told his parents he didn't feel up to the trip. Leading up to it, he had several doctors' appointments, and between that and school, he said he was tired and didn't feel like going. They asked him a few times just to be sure, but he told them he would watch on TV. Kelly traveled to New York with Danny Mulvihill, who had become a good friend.

In the Met Mile, Cody's Wish didn't scare off anyone, with eight horses lined up to take him on at Belmont Park. The field included Zandon, third in the 2022 Kentucky Derby; White Abarrio, who would go on to win the 2023 Breeders' Cup Classic; Dr. Schivel, second in the 2021 Breeders' Cup Sprint; and Slow Down Andy, third to Cody's Wish in the 2022 Breeders' Cup Dirt Mile.

In the eyes of the betting public, however, it was another one-horse race. Cody's Wish was a 3–5 favorite, with the next-closest horse going off at 5–1 odds. Anyone who got a look at him in the paddock could understand why.

When it comes to evaluating Thoroughbreds, appearance matters. As a rule, the horses who look the best run the fastest. And on June 10, 2023, Cody's Wish was the equine male equivalent of a twenty-three-year-old Bo Derek.

"I was walking into the paddock just looking at him," Alvarado said. "He definitely looked the part that day. He looked beautiful."

As they warmed up on the racetrack, the jockey delivered his usual pre-race pep talk to the superstar athlete underneath him.

"Let's do it again. You're the champion. You're faster than these horses. Just do it the right way."

This was the seventh race Alvarado rode Cody's Wish, and, while he had always felt he was sitting on a powerful horse, this was different. If he were an airline pilot, he would have been in the cockpit of the Concorde.

Heading to the gate—where he would start from the rail in the No. 1 post, meaning he would be in there the longest—Cody's Wish was pulling hard, giving Alvarado and the lead pony rider all they could handle. They got him in the gate OK, but with eight other horses to load, Alvarado knew he was in for a battle.

As assistant starter Miguel Ramirez held on to the reins and struggled to stay on the small ledge inside the gate, Alvarado resisted the temptation to dismount, fearing if his horse broke through the gate—a legitimate concern—he would run off and be scratched. The jockey's goggles fogged up due to the exertion, forcing him to pull them down to let in some air.

As the final horse loaded, Cody's Wish started to thrash his head back and forth, up and down, but Ramirez managed to get it relatively straight just before the gate opened. "It wasn't perfect," Alvarado said, "but it was perfect enough."

Cody's Wish broke poorly, as usual, and was eighth after a half-mile, less than four lengths behind leader Hoist The Gold. Still second last going into the turn, Alvarado briefly held back and then swung to the far outside. What happened next was one of the most powerful, electrifying, breathtaking twelve seconds you will ever see on a racetrack, catching the attention of track announcer John Imbriale:

> Cody's Wish is making a big move on the extreme outside. Cody's Wish is picking off horses as they come for the top of the stretch. . . . Here comes Cody's Wish on the outside now to grab the lead. . . . It is Cody's Wish in front. Cody's Wish is drawing away. . . . And this beautiful racing story continues. . . .

A happy Junior Alvarado returns to the winner's circle with Cody's Wish after the 2023 Met Mile. MATHEA KELLEY.

After running a half-mile, Cody's Wish blazed the next eighth-mile in 11.84 seconds—a third of a second faster than he had stormed home to win the Forego at Saratoga. As impressive as it looked on the clock, it was more dazzling on the eyes, simply visually stunning. (Do yourself a favor and google "2023 Met Mile Replay.")

After Cody's Wish crossed the finish line a 3¼-length winner, Kelly Dorman fought back tears in the Belmont Park clubhouse as he clutched the bow tie Cody had worn to the Breeders' Cup. Cody might not have made the trip, but his dad wanted to make sure he could feel his presence, and the bow tie served that purpose.

At home in Richmond, Cody, who had predicted another win, watched on TV and laughed, his version of a screaming, standing ovation. After the winner's circle picture was taken, Alvarado dismounted and handed Kelly two pairs of goggles. "One pair for Cody and one for your daughter," he said. "Give them a hug for me."

Mott had landed his elusive Met Mile, and Team Godolphin was thrilled to give it to him, capturing the race steeped in tradition for the second time (Frosted had won seven years earlier).

"We've been waiting for this day since last fall after the Breeders' Cup," Michael Banahan said. "This is where we wanted to come. I don't know if there's a bigger race in America that we'd like to win. Everyone wants to win the [Kentucky] Derby. I'd rather win this race. You don't get much better than winning the Met Mile."

After the Met Mile, Cody made another sign, this one for Cody's Wish's faithful groom, Ana Urista Hernandez, and he wrote it in Spanish. "Ana, Gracias Por Cuidar el Cody's Wish. [Thank you for taking care of Cody's Wish.] Love, Cody."

With the Met Mile trophy on the way to Jonabell Farm, Mott and Godolphin had to decide where to run Cody's Wish next, but there really was only one logical choice: the Whitney Stakes, named for one of Thoroughbred racing's royal families, at Saratoga Race Course in August.

William Collins Whitney was one of the founders of the Jockey Club and started racing horses in 1898. The family racing operation was carried on by his son, Harry Payne Whitney, and grandson, Cornelius Vanderbilt "Sonny" Whitney, who married Marylou (Schroeder) Hosford in 1958.

Marylou Whitney, who died at age ninety-three in 2019, is arguably one of the most important people in the history of Saratoga Race Course, which dates to 1863. At a time when Saratoga has a total annual attendance of more than one million and fans line up before dawn to get prime backyard spots on big days, it may be hard to conceive that in the 1960s and 1970s it was the least popular of NYRA's three racetracks.

Marylou helped change that by using her status as a socialite and philanthropist to rejuvenate the cultural and social scene in Saratoga Springs and give influential people a reason to visit during the summer racing season. Known as the Grand Dame of Saratoga, she had her share of success as a racehorse owner, with her Birdstone derailing Smarty Jones's Triple Crown bid in the 2004 Belmont Stakes and capturing the Grade 1 Travers Stakes at Saratoga that summer.

Other than the Travers (named for the track's first president, William R. Travers), the Whitney is Saratoga's most important race. The only sticking point for the Cody's Wish connections was the 1⅛-mile distance around two turns. At that point, the horse had run beyond a mile just twice, both losses. He had won at two turns, in the Breeders' Cup Dirt Mile, but in the Whitney he would have to navigate the distance and configuration against top-class horses.

However, it was something of a no-lose proposition. If Cody's Wish were to win the Whitney, Godolphin would consider taking a shot at the 1¼-mile Breeders' Cup Classic in November. If he lost, they could go back to the Dirt Mile.

"Look, we've watched him run. There's a good indication he can do it. But you never know until they do it," Mott said the day before the Whitney, after watching his horse train on a muddy Oklahoma Training Track. "We've got over twenty-four hours to the race, so now it's just like driving defensively on the turnpike. You just have to be careful."

There was plenty of traffic around Mott's barn that Friday morning. Word got out that Cody was in town and was going to visit his horse, guaranteeing a crowd, a group that included the Dormans and Kelly's friend Rick Gregory and his wife, Deata.

The Dormans had driven to upstate New York, stopping at Niagara Falls on the way. They had heard a lot about the magic of Saratoga and were anxious to experience it.

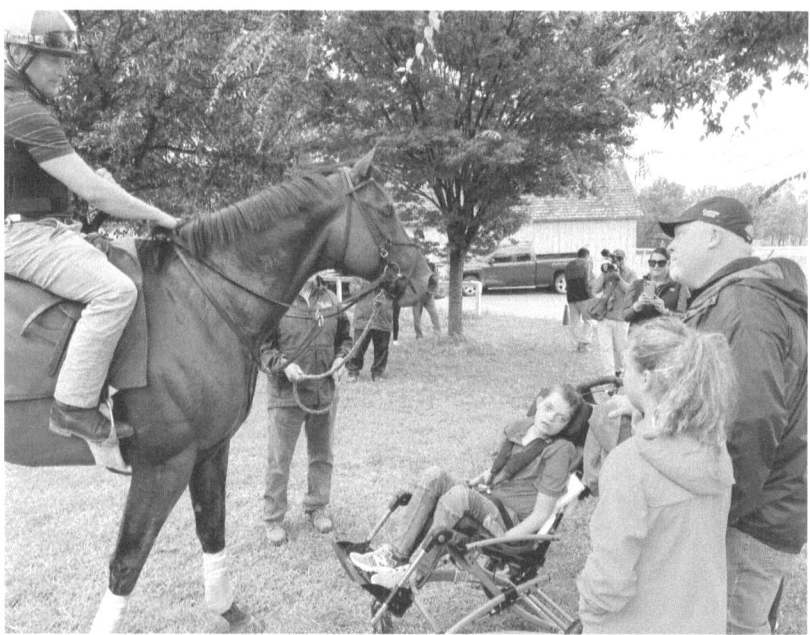

Cody and Cody's Wish drew a crowd at Saratoga the morning before the 2023 Whitney. PAUL HALLORAN.

"They told me as great as Belmont was, the intensity up here is off the charts," Kelly said over dinner one night at Pennell's, a popular Italian restaurant a few miles from the track. "Now I know what they mean."

On Friday morning, Kelly and Leslie stationed Cody's wheelchair in front of Cody's Wish's stall and, for several minutes, the two friends—one an equine superstar and the other an embodiment of courage and resilience—simply looked at each other.

That night, the Dormans were guests of honor at a barbecue a few miles from the track. Cody was, as always, a rock star, meeting a group of veteran horseplayers genuinely touched to be in his presence. There were deep, lasting relationships born on Beacon Hill Drive August 4, 2023—bonds that will never be broken.

On Whitney Day, the Dormans sat in the 1863 Club, a dining area near the start of the clubhouse turn. The race was not scheduled to go off until 5:44 p.m., so there was plenty of time to soak up the atmosphere of a spectacular Saratoga Saturday.

Two races before the Whitney, Godolphin had the favorite in the Test Stakes, Pretty Mischievous, who won the Kentucky Oaks the day before the Kentucky Derby. Also in the Test was Maple Leaf Mel, an undefeated three-year-old filly owned by NFL Hall of Fame coach Bill Parcells and trained by the horse's namesake, Melanie Giddings, a stage 4 cancer survivor in her first full year training on her own.

Under Joel Rosario, who rode Cody's Wish to his maiden win in 2021, Maple Leaf Mel took control from the outset and led at every call. Approaching the finish line, Rosario sneaked a look behind him to confirm there was no threat. Parcells got up from his box seat and started to make his way down the stairs toward the winner's circle to celebrate his first Grade 1 win as an owner.

Then unthinkable tragedy struck.

Less than ten yards from the wire, Maple Leaf Mel went down, ejecting Rosario, who hit the dirt hard and rolled across the finish line. The gray filly, a few strides from victory, suffered a catastrophic injury to her right front leg. When she tried to get up, she fell again, unable to put any pressure on the fractured limb. Within several minutes, Maple Leaf Mel, a filly with unlimited potential and a compelling backstory, was euthanized on the track, behind a screen intended to shield fans' eyes. It was horrifying.

Just like that, nothing else that happened at Saratoga that day would matter quite as much. It's hard to imagine many worse moments in the history of one of the country's oldest sporting venues. The collective air

Artist Jocelyn Russell met the Dormans when she brought her magnificent Secretariat statue to Saratoga. Her Cody's Wish statue was unveiled in October 2025. DORMAN FAMILY.

was sucked out of the track the way it leaves a balloon when you release your grip on its neck.

Pretty Mischievous won by default, but the Godolphin team wanted no part of anything resembling a celebration, because on this day there was nothing to be happy about, even winning a $500,000 Grade 1 race.

"I don't know what to say. I don't think words can describe it. It feels like nothing," Pretty Mischievous's trainer, Brendan Walsh, told Sean Clancy of *The Saratoga Special* for a story that won a media Eclipse Award in the News Writing category. "I just feel terrible for them. For the filly. A champion like her, the way she ran. Nobody wants to win a race like that."

Watching the demise of Maple Leaf Mel was like taking a Mike Tyson gut punch, but horse racing is a show-must-go-on business, and an hour later, when the Dormans started to head to the paddock to see Cody's Wish, the 1863 Club erupted in applause.

Cody's Wish walked by Cody on the way to be saddled, taking a quick look at his friend. When Alvarado arrived in the paddock, he caught sight of a horse who didn't resemble the equine beauty who had greeted him at Belmont. To Alvarado, Cody's Wish looked like everyone felt after the Maple Leaf Mel tragedy. On the track, the jockey's suspicions were confirmed.

"I don't think he was himself," Alvarado said. "That's a horse who's full of energy all the time. That day, he just was dull. I warmed him up more than I normally warm him up because I never felt that he had good energy underneath me."

When it was time to go into the gate, Cody's Wish wanted no part of it, something that had not happened before. Sure, he could be a problem once loaded, but he was more likely to be fighting to get in than needing to be coaxed.

Finally loaded in the gate, he was no altar boy, though not as surly as at some of his previous races. That, too, turned out to be a bad sign. Starting from the far outside in the six-horse field, he broke awkwardly and was still last after a half-mile. With three furlongs to run, Alvarado asked his horse to pick it up. The response was muted, Cody's Wish advancing into fourth off the turn as White Abarrio, whom he had soundly beaten in the Met Mile, romped to a six-length win. Cody's Wish won a photo finish for third.

Alvarado's worst fears were realized.

"By the three-quarter pole [one-third of the way into the race], I already knew I had no chance whatsoever. Zero chance," he said. "He just wasn't traveling well. He wasn't in trouble or anything like that. He just wasn't there for me. I could tell he was just going through the motions. I couldn't get any feeling out of him. Even though at some point he started picking off some horses, I knew I had no chance."

Kelly Dorman theorized that Cody's Wish might have somehow picked up on the dour vibe resulting from the Maple Leaf Mel tragedy and that it affected his performance. You may think that's a reach, but with this story, be cynical at your own risk.

A logical explanation would be to attribute the loss to the horse not wanting to run that far. But while you can't dispute the result, Alvarado will always believe there was more to it.

"We can use the distance as an excuse, but that day whether it was six furlongs, seven furlongs, a mile, it doesn't make a difference," he said. "There was nothing physically wrong with him, but it just wasn't his day and he wasn't going to win. You could see it in his eyes. He was a different animal."

Saratoga has a reputation as the Graveyard of Champions—which, tragically, had gone from metaphorical to literal earlier that day—where even the immortal Secretariat was not immune to being upset fifty years earlier. For the first time, Cody had to leave the winner's circle without posing for a photo.

Perhaps it was the Maple Leaf Mel incident putting everything into perspective, but the Dormans refused to allow their first trip to Saratoga to be ruined by a loss in a horse race. They stopped by Mott's barn Sunday morning to say goodbye to Cody's Wish, and Kylie got to ride Mott's stable pony, Bugsy.

"The impact that Saratoga made on our family will remain at the top of the list for the rest of our lives," they wrote in an open letter to the Saratoga Race Course community. "Who knows what lies ahead in the chapter that Cody and Cody's Wish will write next."

With the Breeders' Cup Classic off the table, the target became a repeat in the Breeders' Cup Dirt Mile, that year scheduled to be held on the West Coast at Santa Anita, in what would be the final race of Cody's Wish's career. Going to Saratoga was an away game; heading to California would be a legitimate road trip, and the Dormans wouldn't miss it for the world.

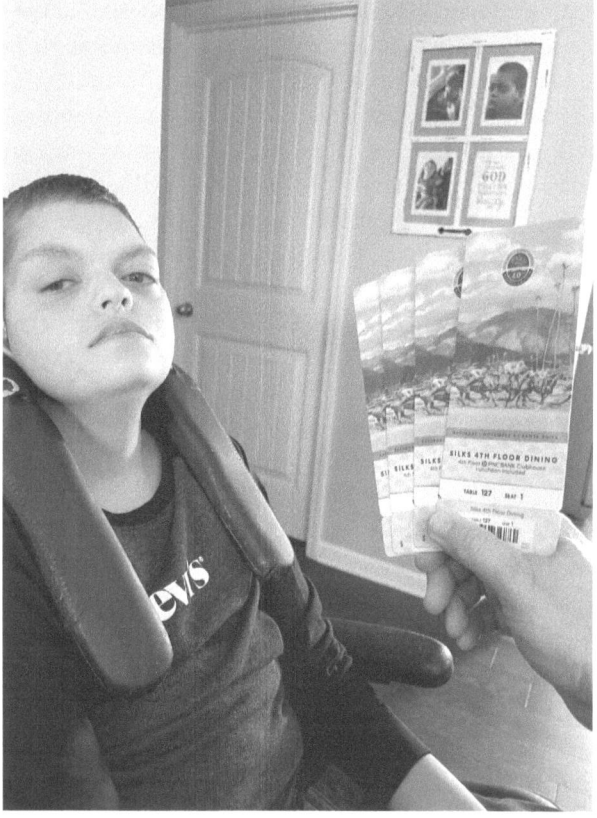

California, here he comes! DORMAN FAMILY.

15

California Dreamin'

IT WAS THE MIDDLE OF THE NIGHT, AND CODY WAS RESTLESS. THE DORMANS were staying at the Le Méridien hotel close to Santa Anita Park, host track for the 2023 Breeders' Cup in Arcadia, California. With Cody's Wish set for his last race, they weren't about to let a twenty-two-hundred-mile trip—and all the challenges that went with it—stand in the way of Cody being there for his best friend's swan song.

The Dorman family traveled to the West Coast on Tuesday—Halloween—so they could get settled in before the whirlwind of activity that awaited.

The trip went relatively smoothly, after a delay getting out of Lexington for de-icing almost caused them to miss their connection in Atlanta.

"We were going through the Atlanta airport picking off people," Kelly Dorman said. "Looked like Cody's Wish coming down the stretch."

The trip to California was the second cross-country sojourn for Cody. A year earlier, the family had traveled to Arizona for Cody to receive the Big Sport of Turfdom Award from the Turf Publicists of America, given to someone who enhances coverage of Thoroughbred racing through cooperation with the media and racing publicists. It was the first time Kelly, Cody, and Kylie had ever been on an airplane.

In accepting the award, Cody thanked the University of Arizona Race Track Industry Program gathering for supporting him and Cody's Wish.

"I am so thankful that this makes people smile and how it has touched your hearts," he said through his tablet. "God bless all of you. Each of you inspire me in the same way that Cody's Wish does. Hopefully we can see each other at the track next year."

That trip was a learning experience when it came to traveling by air with Cody. By the time they packed all of his medical equipment, they had filled three extra suitcases. A year later, they were much better prepared, thanks to a Santa Anita executive who made it her mission to make their lives easier.

Amy Zimmerman, a track vice president and NBC producer who was tuned in to the Cody story, arranged for them to ship as much as they could in advance: feeding bags and pump, formula, and anything else that could be sent. She even went out and bought a new IV pole so they would not have to bring one.

"I really didn't do much, just helped them get what they needed for Cody to get out to Santa Anita," she said. "My son was born at two pounds, two and a half ounces. I know the terror, and it was by God's grace that he didn't have any lasting complications. So if there's anything that I, or by extension, Santa Anita, could do to make life easier for this family, it was going to be done."

It was around 2 a.m. on Wednesday when Cody woke his parents. So much for getting a good night's sleep before the long week ahead. Leslie, one eye open, retrieved the tablet so Cody could tell them what was on his mind.

"Wake me up at 7," he told his parents. "I want to go to the track."

Leslie made a half-hearted attempt to talk him out of it, but she knew once Cody made up his mind, he was at least as stubborn as the average teenager, if not more. The Dormans pulled into Santa Anita at 8 a.m.—a reserved parking spot waiting, thanks to Zimmerman—in time to catch morning training.

They went out to the rail, and a horse standing on the stretch turn caught their eye, at first due to his massive size and then by the symmetrical white diamond on his forehead. It was as if Cody knew exactly when to get there, just as Cody's Wish was set to train. It may be reasonable to chalk that up to coincidence—the Dormans had no idea when the horse would be on the track—but with this story, the happenstance train had long left the station.

The first scheduled event on their calendar was the National Turf Writers and Broadcasters annual awards dinner that night, where Team Cody's Wish was receiving the Mr. Fitz Award for typifying the spirit of racing. The turf writers' dinner was held at Altadena Town & Country Club, a first-class facility that sadly fell victim to the California wildfires in January 2025. Cody shared the spotlight with the other human connections who played an integral role in transforming this fairy tale into reality: mainly the Godolphin team, Bill Mott and his assistants, and Cody's parents and sister.

Cody prepared remarks in advance, telling the room full of writers and broadcasters, "I love everyone on the team with all my heart. They all work hard to see my wish and their wishes come true."

Heading to the barn area at Santa Anita on Thursday afternoon, as Kelly pushed Cody, something he saw in the distance made him stop. There was someone in a chair similar to Cody's, but because Kelly was in the sun and that person was in the shade, all he could make out was a silhouette. From a distance it looked like Cody.

Carson Jost was the man in the chair, with his father, Wade, holding it and his mother, Kim, off to the side. Carson and Cody had two things in common, the chances of which were infinitesimal.

The thirty-one-year-old Carson also had a Grade 1–winning horse named for him—Carson's Run, owned by Stephen Bouchey and West Point Thoroughbreds, a syndicate led by Terry Finley. Wade Jost was Finley's classmate at the United States Military Academy, and they had remained close in the thirty-five years since. Finley had been talking about naming a horse for Carson for more than twenty years. Attending a classmate's funeral in 2023 prompted him to make it happen.

West Point paid $170,000 for a two-year-old son of Cupid in April, and the newly named Carson's Run won his debut at Saratoga in July. Trainer Christophe Clement immediately threw him into the deep end, and the colt responded with a second-place finish in a Grade 3 stakes race at Saratoga and a win in a Grade 1 at Woodbine in Canada. That earned him a trip to California for the Breeders' Cup Juvenile Turf.

Cody and Carson shared far more than simply having racehorses named after them. Carson was also born with Wolf-Hirschhorn syndrome. Based on the rarity of the genetic disease, it was almost statistically inconceivable there would be two people with Wolf-Hirschhorn at the same racetrack at the same time, both to watch horses named for them compete in the most important races of the year. At one point, as Cody leaned to his left and Carson to his right, their heads were almost touching. It was an emotional encounter for their parents, who didn't often get the chance to be with others who traveled the same seemingly Sisyphean journey.

"Sometimes you feel like you're on an island. You can't see anything out there past your own situation," Kelly told Wade Jost. "But these young men teach us every day. They open doors in the back of your heart. It hit me so hard realizing we would be getting to meet your family and Carson. When we were walking up through here, I turned and said to Leslie, 'My God, look at him. He's sitting in that chair just like Cody does.' It took us a little longer to get here because we had to dry out a little bit."

Cody met a new friend, Carson Jost, on the Santa Anita backstretch. PAUL HALLORAN.

As the fathers talked and hugged and fought back tears with varying levels of success, Wade shared with Kelly something deeply personal that brought him solace as he watched his son grow into his thirties. The crux of it was that God-fearing people have as their ultimate goal an invitation to Heaven when they die, presuming they live their life accordingly.

Pointing to Carson and Cody, Wade told Kelly those two had nothing to worry about. To put it in gambling terms, they were mortal locks to win the ultimate race. "That does give me comfort," Wade said. "We're the ones who have to worry about making it there."

It's reasonable to believe parents such as the Josts and Dormans might have the inside track, too.

The mothers, Leslie and Kim, also had a chance to connect and commiserate, comparing notes on seizure medication and brittle bones. They learned they had similar attitudes when it came to how they chose to let their sons live, evidenced by their presence at Santa Anita.

"When he was younger we went everywhere," Kim told Leslie, "because, first of all, they told us when he was born, and I'm sure you probably got the same spiel, 'You probably won't bring him home and he won't make it past infancy and then he won't make it past toddlerhood.' He's thirty-one years old. We said, 'OK, if this is what we're going to do, we're going to do it right and we're going to show him as much of the world as we can.'"

Kim admitted it had become harder to transport Carson as he got older, which made this trip even more significant. Meeting Cody and his family was a bonus.

"I think it's wonderful," Kim said, "because we're riding down the same road and there's not too many who have been down that road."

After about an hour, the Josts and the Dormans went separate ways, vowing to remain in touch and wishing each other luck with the horses who had brought so much joy to their sons. The Dormans would root for Carson's Run on Friday, and the Josts would be cheering on Cody's Wish on Saturday.

Having been in California only forty-eight hours, Leslie and Kelly already felt emotionally drained—and the race was still two days away. Cody knew this was Cody's Wish's last race, and he expressed mixed emotions: sad he would not get to see him run anymore, but excited to visit him at Jonabell Farm and even more anxious to see his babies hit the track, four years down the line.

To some degree, 2023 was a bonus, since it would not have been surprising if Godolphin had retired the horse after his Breeders' Cup win the year before. That possibility was eliminated when Kelly got a call from Godolphin's Dan Pride the morning after the 2022 Breeders' Cup to let him know Cody's Wish would run as a five-year-old.

Now there really was a finite endpoint to this story, or at least the racing chapters. The 2023 Dirt Mile would be the last time Cody's Wish entered a starting gate—good news for those stuck in there with him—and the final opportunity for Cody to give him a pre-race pep talk.

A few hours after meeting Carson and his parents, the Dormans went to visit the big horse in the barn area. Mott brought out Cody's Wish, and, on cue, he walked toward Cody and lowered his head toward his lap, the best friends locking eyes as they had so many times before. Mott helped Cody feed him a carrot, and it was hard to tell who enjoyed that most among the three of them.

Cody gazed at the horse, and while only he could know what he was thinking—and would be saying if his voice were not trapped inside his frail, ravaged body—perhaps it was something like "OK, big boy, one more time. I'm going to be there for you just like you have been there for me. Let's go out on top."

Based on how he was training since arriving at Santa Anita, Cody's Wish had every intention of finishing as a winner. He bounced back

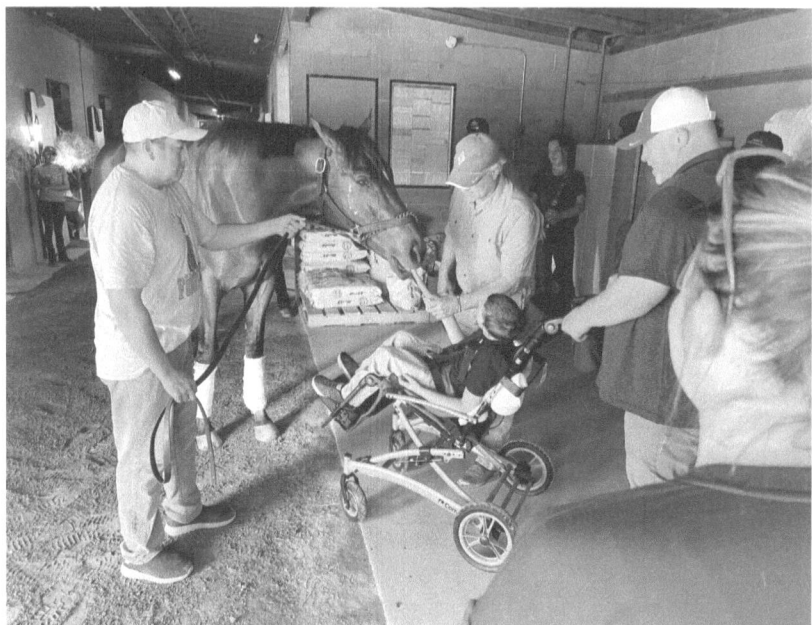

With the help of Bill Mott, Cody fed his friend a carrot two days before the final race, the 2023 Breeders' Cup Dirt Mile. PAUL HALLORAN.

from the Whitney loss with a workmanlike win in the Grade 2 Vosburgh Stakes at Aqueduct October 1, a race for which Mott did not have him 100 percent cranked, but he did enough to get by, winning by 1½ lengths after Alvarado got him involved in the race much earlier than usual. They needed to make sure the Saratoga loss was an anomaly, regardless of the reason (distance/two turns/off day) and that the horse would be ready for one last run.

Arriving in California ten days before the Breeders' Cup, Cody's Wish had his final timed workout Sunday, October 29, going a half-mile in a crisp 47⅕ seconds. As the week went on, he became more aggressive in the morning, giving exercise rider Neil Poznansky all he could handle. It got to the point that Mott was starting to get concerned that the horse might be too keyed up, so the two days before the race he switched the routine, sending Cody's Wish to the less crowded training track and having Poznansky jog him the wrong way around, in an effort to trick him into thinking a race was not imminent.

Friday was another long day at the track for the Dormans, who came out for morning training and stayed for day one of the Breeders' Cup. Carson's Run drew the far outside post in the fourteen-horse Juvenile Turf, significantly decreasing his chances. He was unfortunately never a factor and finished ninth.

At the hotel that night, Cody again woke his parents in the middle of the night—2:32 a.m., to be exact—and asked for his tablet. He had something to tell them and Kylie, and it could not wait. His message was short and very sweet:

"Thank you for taking me here."

It was going to be an early start to the day anyway, with the Dirt Mile scheduled to go off at 11:30 a.m. local time. After they put on their Breeders' Cup best—Leslie and Kylie wearing blue dresses, Kelly a blue suit, and Cody dark, pinstriped pants, matching vest, and his lucky bow tie—they headed downstairs in the elevator to leave for the racetrack. When the doors opened in the lobby, the first two people they saw were Junior and Kelly Alvarado.

You never know who you're going to meet in the hotel lobby at the Breeders' Cup, as the Dormans and Alvarados found out. DORMAN FAMILY.

Alvarado felt more pressure than ever before a race, even after notching his second Breeders' Cup win the day before when he piloted Just F Y I to victory in the Juvenile Fillies. After 13,091 mounts in North America and 2,071 wins to that point, you might think he would be immune to anything other than the normal big-race butterflies. Think again.

"I couldn't eat the day before," the jockey said. "I was hungry, but every time I thought about the race, my appetite would go away. I remember my wife telling me, 'You need to eat. You need to be strong. You know the horse is strong, you need to ride strong.' But every time I thought about how important this race was, I just lost my appetite. The only thing that I had for probably twenty or thirty hours was coffee."

Cody's prowess as a prognosticator had been almost perfect, so Alvarado figured he would ask whether an official prediction had been released. Kelly told him Cody had indeed forecast another Breeders' Cup win.

"I thought it was going to be a relief to hear that, but it actually built up more pressure," Alvarado said, though he resigned himself to accepting whatever fate had in store. "I was like, 'OK, if it's meant to be, it's meant to be.' I just have to go out there and do my job."

Once they got to the track, the Dormans didn't bother going to their seats, since the Dirt Mile was the third race on the card and they wanted to be in the paddock as soon as the horses for the second race headed to the track. They were approached by a steady flow of well-wishers, all of them anxious to share how they had been touched by the story.

It was not yet 11 a.m., and the emotion meter was already off the charts.

Joel Rosario, who rode Cody's Wish three times early in his career and was aboard for his first win in 2021—the first time Cody saw the horse run in person—was on the way to the paddock for the second race of the day when he spotted the Dormans. He stopped on a dime and rerouted to greet them.

"I'm glad I was a part of all that," Rosario said one afternoon at Saratoga. "I really cannot explain it to you. It was really emotional and really special. That horse had a real connection with Cody, and for me to be part of it was amazing."

Kelly and Leslie were thrilled to spend a few minutes with him. "We've always loved Joel," Kelly said. "He's a class act."

As the horses were being saddled for the Dirt Mile, Kelly told NBC's Nick Luck he was nervous, proud, and in awe of the impact his son and Cody's Wish had made on so many people. Kylie gently rubbed her brother's head with the love and devotion of a sister who might not have lived in the same spotlight but knew her brother was a shining star.

Cody, looking drained from the hectic week, reached out for Luck's hand as Kelly confirmed his son had told them the night before this story would have a happy ending.

Nine horses were entered in the Dirt Mile, but two scratches left a field of seven. Cody's Wish was No. 3 in the program—appropriately wearing the blue saddlecloth in keeping with the dress code of the day—occupying the gate second closest to the rail after the scratches. The notorious bad boy behaved OK once they loaded him, pleasantly surprising his jockey.

"He started acting up a little bit, but it wasn't as terrible as he normally is," Alvarado said. "He was actually standing pretty good, for him."

After the gate opened, Cody's Wish was in his familiar spot at the back of the pack within a few strides. The good news was National Treasure, who had won the Preakness Stakes in May, and Skippylongstocking went fast early—22.51 seconds for the first quarter-mile—with National Treasure winning the battle for the lead.

Alvarado had Cody's Wish last heading into the first turn, but by the time they hit the backstretch he had improved his position to sixth, almost nine lengths behind. Flavien Prat got National Treasure to settle down and managed to run the second quarter-mile exactly one second slower than the first, a significant development for a horse who would have to try to hold off a fast-closing Cody's Wish in the stretch.

There wasn't much change in position down the backstretch. National Treasure was a length ahead of Skippylongstocking, who was a length in front of Shirl's Bee. As they approached the far turn, Alvarado decided it was time to go. He sensed the pace was quick enough and he liked what he felt underneath him. He didn't want to move too soon, but he was determined not to leave his horse with too much to do in the stretch. Not today.

"By the five-eighths pole, I moved my hands a little bit just to know how much horse I had," he said, "and he quickly jumped into the bridle. I was like, 'OK, I'm good.' I just had to wait, start making my move little by little. I had to be paying attention, very aware of what was happening in front so I can know when to move. I didn't want to move too late. I didn't want to move too soon."

As they went around the turn, Alvarado took Cody's Wish off the rail to pass a tiring Zozos and then went back to the inside, his spurt catching the eye of Larry Collmus, again calling the race for NBC.

"Cody's Wish is coming now . . ." Collmus said. "Junior Alvarado and Cody's Wish are on the move."

As they approached the stretch, Cody's Wish was third and gaining. Alvarado could have opted to swing to the outside at that point, but he was aware that National Treasure was a tough customer on the lead and didn't want to lose any more ground than necessary. That led him to stay inside of Skippylongstocking and make a between-horses move as he took aim at National Treasure.

"The only two races that he had won before that, he was on the lead," Alvarado said of National Treasure. "When you get to him, you just don't go by. If he goes slow, if he goes fast, he will put up a fight. He wasn't a horse who was going to get tired easily. I was very aware of that."

In the announcer's booth, Collmus picked up on Alvarado's advance.

"Here comes Cody's Wish alongside National Treasure," Collmus said, his voice rising to meet the moment.

Cody's Wish got his head in front at the sixteenth pole, and the way he finished his races, you would have expected him to run away in the final half-furlong. But National Treasure—the grandson of Medaglia d'Oro, the elder statesman of stallions at Godolphin's Jonabell Farm, where Cody's Wish was headed after this race—dug in, just as Alvarado thought he would.

The horses were virtually inseparable in the final strides, exchanging a few bumps as they lunged for the wire. At one point, it looked as if National Treasure might come back on the inside to pull off a seismic upset—not because he was some hopeless longshot (he was the third betting choice at 9–2 odds) but due to the possibility of denying this story its fairy-tale ending.

"Cody's Wish and National Treasure coming down to the line," Collmus shouted. "Fighting back, National Treasure . . ."

As they hit the wire, it looked like Cody's Wish was a nose in front, but even Collmus, who has a knack of calling photo finishes correctly (check out the 2016 Breeders' Cup Distaff), hedged his bet.

"Oh, Cody's Wish, I think he won it by a nose on the wire over National Treasure," he told viewers. "Thank you, Cody, and thank you, Cody's Wish."

In the winner's circle, there was joyous bedlam. Kelly kissed Cody on the head and gave Dan Pride a bear hug, Leslie celebrated with a writer who had become family, and Kylie cried tears of joy. The unofficial order of finish was posted: 3-9-6.

About a hundred miles from the final resting place of Frank Sinatra, who once sang about the possibility of fairy tales coming true, this one got the happy ending it deserved.

"When you put Cody and Cody's Wish and the good Lord in something like that . . ." Kelly told Nick Luck, fighting back tears. "I'm sorry, I

National Treasure was a tough customer, but Cody's Wish would not be denied in his quest for a second Breeders' Cup Dirt Mile win. JOHN VOORHEES/ECLIPSE SPORTSWIRE/BREEDERS' CUP.

can't talk and cry at the same time. There's no quit in this horse and there's no quit in that young man over there."

Alvarado pulled up Cody's Wish on the backstretch and reversed direction for a final triumphant return to the winner's circle, where Cody was waiting for his best friend. It was a perfect climax to a story that began on a farm in Kentucky five years earlier and had delivered enough suspense to last multiple lifetimes.

So many times, the clock strikes midnight on Cinderella stories, but not this day. This drama, a love story at its core and a spellbinding example of the triumph of the human spirit, was concluding the only way it could.

Or was it?

16

Hold All Tickets

A FEW DAYS BEFORE THE BREEDERS' CUP, HORSES LINED UP OUTSIDE TRAINER Bob Baffert's barn on the Santa Anita backstretch, waiting to head to the paddock for schooling, a dry run for the race-day experience.

Baffert's barn is close to the stable gate, so he had an up-close look at a number of horses who would be running over the weekend. One in particular caught his eye.

"Who's that?" he asked an assistant.

"That's Cody's Wish."

Someone said to Baffert, "You have to run against *him*?"

The Hall of Fame trainer found himself in the odd position of coming into the race with a classic winner, National Treasure, and feeling like a longshot against Cody's Wish.

"When you get to the Breeders' Cup, it's been a long year, and some horses might be tailing off a little bit," Baffert said. "Some of them have already peaked. But he looked tremendous. Big, strong, good-looking horse. Wow. I told one of my assistants, 'We might need a bigger boat,' like the guy in the *Jaws* movie."

Baffert was far from ready to concede, no matter how imposing Cody's Wish—or any horse—looked. In the Breeders' Cup, they're all tough.

"The Breeders' Cup races are so hard to win. It's the best of the best," Baffert said. "You have to be really good that day. It's a very important day for all of us because the whole world is watching. So we all have our horses as ready as we can get them."

The Kentucky Derby is the highest-profile race of the year, but its unparalleled popularity can be attributed to the pomp and circumstance, fancy clothes, and classic mint juleps as much as to the twenty horses who load into the Churchill Downs starting gate on the first Saturday in May.

With the Breeders' Cup, the focus is squarely on the fourteen world championship races held over the course of two days, though the marketing people have done a credible job of pumping up the "wow" factor, enlisting the services of "ambassadors" such as actresses Elizabeth Banks and Kate Upton and professional athletes Alex Bregman and Gary Player.

The NFL season culminates with the Super Bowl, Major League Baseball the World Series, and horse racing the Breeders' Cup. However, because racing is not really a team sport, Baffert has a better comparison.

"The Breeders' Cup is our Olympics," he said. "The classics [Triple Crown races] are different. It's all about one group of horses, three-year-olds. But in the Breeders' Cup, it's the best of the best in all the different divisions."

Baffert has had more horses cross the finish line first in the Kentucky Derby than any trainer in history, though the disqualification of 2021 winner Medina Spirit due to a failed drug test officially left him tied with Ben Jones with six wins in the Run for the Roses. Baffert won the Triple Crown with American Pharoah in 2015—the first such victory in thirty-seven years—and Justify in 2018. Heading into the 2023 Breeders' Cup, he had won eighteen of the championship races. (A win in 2025 gave him twenty-one, tied for the all-time lead with Irish legend Aidan O'Brien.)

The 2023 Dirt Mile came with several factors in Baffert's favor:

- Home-track advantage—National Treasure had run four races at Santa Anita, with three top-three finishes; Cody's Wish had never ventured west of Kentucky.
- Running style—The Southern California tracks are typically more conducive to horses with early speed. National Treasure preferred to be on or near the lead, while Cody's Wish, in his last six races, had run against forty horses and been in front of only four of them after a quarter-mile.
- Track configuration—At Santa Anita, a mile is a two-turn race and, while Cody's Wish was successful in a two-turn Dirt Mile at Keeneland in 2022, he was clearly a much better one-turn horse due to his one-run, fast-closing style. Also, at 990 feet, the Santa Anita stretch is shorter than almost all major racetracks.

Put it all together, and Baffert knew National Treasure had a fighting chance, though he didn't anticipate that materializing in the literal sense.

"Coming into the race, I felt my horse was doing really, really well," he said. "It was a matter of who's going to get the trip. Cody's Wish comes from off the pace. And sometimes at these tracks, speed wins. So that was the advantage that we had over Cody's Wish. He's going to have to come catch us."

In his pre-race discussions with Flavien Prat, a world-class rider originally from France who set a record for stakes wins in 2024 and won the Eclipse Award as top jockey in North America, Baffert laid out the strategy.

"I think our speed is our weapon. Let's just get him out there and let him roll," he told Prat, who followed the instructions to a T. As the horses went around the first turn with National Treasure leading and Cody's Wish second last, Baffert liked what he saw.

"I'm feeling good," he said. "We're good. And I'm looking back and I see Cody's Wish, because always, when I watch a race, I watch my horse and the horse I have to beat. He's way back there. OK, this is good."

The trainer's outlook remained positive as the horses ran down the backstretch.

"He's out there and he's doing it the right way," Baffert said. "I look at Cody's Wish; [Alvarado's] starting to scrub on him [asking him to pick up the pace]. He's starting to move. And I'm thinking we're still looking good. And they turned to straighten out for home and I see Cody's Wish is making up ground, but there's no way he's going to catch us. I think we're home."

Once Cody's Wish took aim at National Treasure, Baffert braced for a stirring stretch duel, pleading for the finish line.

"Where's the wire?" he said of his reaction. "You're looking for the wire at that point."

When the two equine stars crossed the line, Baffert knew National Treasure had been nosed.

"He nailed us, right on the wire," he said. "I felt like my horse ran a winning race. Both horses ran winning races."

There can be only one winner, and it almost immediately occurred to Baffert that if there is such a thing as a "good" loss, this qualified.

"You know, some things are bigger than winning, and nobody on our team was disappointed with the outcome," he said. "It was a great race. It was just one of those things where Cody's Wish willed himself to win that race. I've had horses like that. They just have so much will. They find a way to get there. And that's what makes them great horses."

If Baffert were going to get beat, Cody's Wish was the right horse, and not just because of the heartwarming story of Cody Dorman. He had no problem losing to a horse owned by Godolphin and Sheikh Mohammed, whom he credits with saving his life.

In 2012, Baffert flew to Dubai to saddle two horses on the Dubai World Cup card—nine races worth a total of $27.25 million at the time. He didn't feel well on the sixteen-hour flight to the Middle East and was worse when he landed, experiencing chest pain. Attributing it to a long day of travel, he went to bed.

His phone rang at 3:30 in the morning on Monday, March 26. It was a call congratulating him on a horse he trained—Princess Arabella—winning the Sunland Park Oaks in New Mexico, just over the border from El Paso, Texas. That race was run at 5:16 p.m. local time on March 25, which was the middle of the night in Dubai.

After Baffert got the good news and watched the replay, he realized the chest pain had not subsided. He chalked it up to indigestion, a diagnosis his wife, Jill, summarily dismissed. She did what many would do in that situation—pulled up WebMD.com—and asked him a few questions.

"Does your neck hurt?"

"No."

"Does your left arm hurt?"

"My God, my left arm is killing me."

"You're having a heart attack."

At 4 a.m., in a hotel more than eighty-three hundred miles from home, Baffert wasn't sure what to do, so he called an American veterinarian he knew worked for Sheikh Mohammed. Next thing he knew, Baffert was being taken by ambulance to a hospital, where a cardiac surgeon inserted three stents in two arteries, which were 100 and 90 percent blocked, meaning he got to the hospital just in time and the immediate diagnosis and procedure were critical to his surviving.

That night, Baffert received a visitor who had heads turning.

"Sheikh Mo showed up at nine o'clock to visit me. That was pretty cool," Baffert said. "When he left, the nurses came in and asked, 'Who are you? His Highness has never come to the hospital.' I told them I was just a horse trainer. That's all I do. But that's the guy he is. The care was excellent."

Baffert got out of the hospital in time for the stakes races, which did not go well. He ran sixth in the Golden Shaheen with The Factor and twelfth in the $10 million World Cup with Game On Dude, a horse partly owned by former New York Yankees manager Joe Torre. All the connections were dejected, but, while Baffert wasn't thrilled with flying a third of the way around the world to lose, he appreciated being alive to see those defeats.

Eleven years later, he was more than OK with losing by a nose to a horse owned by Sheikh Mohammed, especially this horse.

Hold All Tickets 161

In the winner's circle, Kelly Dorman was starting a TV interview when Santa Anita track announcer Frank Mirahmadi announced something many of the revelers did not immediately pick up on.

"Ladies and gentlemen, there is going to be a stewards' inquiry into the stretch run," Mirahmadi said, adding that it involved the first two finishers.

The California Horse Racing Board stewards are authorized to post an inquiry if they feel that there may have been a foul that affected the outcome of the race.

According to CHRB Rule No. 1699:

During the running of the race:

(a) A horse shall not interfere with any other horse. Interference is defined as bumping, impeding, forcing or floating in or out or otherwise causing any other horse to lose stride, ground, momentum or position.

(b) A horse which interferes with another as defined in subsection (a) may be disqualified and placed behind the horse so interfered with if, in the opinion of the Stewards, the horse interfered with was not at fault and due to the interference lost the opportunity for a better placing.

Cody's Wish and National Treasure had bumped three times in the last hundred yards. If the stewards determined that Cody's Wish was

Things got physical in the stretch, causing the stewards to post an inquiry.
MATHEA KELLEY.

culpable for the contact and that it cost National Treasure the win, they would be obligated to disqualify him.

Could that really happen?

As they galloped out after the race, Prat told Alvarado he was going to claim foul, but the stewards had already posted the inquiry indicating they were going to take a closer look either way. Alvarado was confident Cody's Wish didn't initiate the contact, even if he was a willing participant in the roughhousing.

"He came out first. It was like a light brush," Alvarado said of National Treasure. "I can feel my horse trying to go into a fistfight. He tried to throw his body back at him. I don't want to do this right now. We're already in front. I don't want to be in this bumping thing. I want to win. And I could feel that he still wanted to win, but he wanted to try to go after the horse. He wanted to lean on him. He wanted to push him."

Including his body weight, equipment, and tack, Alvarado was carrying 126 pounds that day. In an instant it became his job to convince an eleven-hundred-pound, agitated Thoroughbred that discretion is the better part of valor.

"Maybe any other race, any other horse, I would feel the same way and try to go after him and bump back," he said, "but I was so close to the wire. I just wanted to get there first. I knew I had him."

He was aware that when he got back to the winner's circle, he would need to convince the stewards nothing he did warranted a disqualification. And in the time it took to return the verdict, he could think only the worst.

"Sick feeling. Extremely sick feeling," he said. "Then I start thinking, 'It's Bob Baffert. This is his home track. He wins all the races here. Is that going to help him?' It was just a terrible feeling."

In American racing, when there is a stewards' inquiry or a claim of foul, the jockeys speak individually to the stewards on a telephone stationed in the winner's circle. There are those who think this is a waste of time that introduces the possibility that a jockey with better lawyer skills could have an advantage, while one who may struggle with the English language could be penalized.

In this case, you had a Frenchman and a Venezuelan who had been in the United States for eight and sixteen years, respectively, both of whom spoke English just fine. Prat got on the phone first; then it was Alvarado's turn to speak to Grant Baker, one of the three California stewards overseeing the races that day, sharing the booth with lead steward Kim Sawyer and Luis Jauregui.

Alvarado told Baker that National Treasure initiated the contact—an assertion supported by video—and he thought Cody's Wish might have been knocked off balance by the original bump. He said he tried to keep riding straight, knowing his horse had already put his head in front.

Then he was asked the question he was hoping to hear.

"Do you think that horse was going to go by you again?"

Alvarado was emphatic in his response; he believed with all his heart the veracity of what he said.

"No. We could have been in that battle for another eighth of a mile and he wasn't going to pass me," Alvarado told the steward. "He was going to stay with me, but he wasn't going to pass me. Once I got my horse in front I wasn't going to let the other horse go by again."

Sawyer, a steward with more than twenty years' experience, explained that she and Baker typically view the races on large-screen TVs, while Jauregui watches live, through binoculars. As it unfolds, if they see something that might warrant a closer look, they note it out loud in real time. Once the horses cross the finish line, they decide whether to post an inquiry, usually within a minute or two. In the case of the $1 million Breeders' Cup Dirt Mile, the contact in the stretch made it an easy decision.

"We had to get involved in it," Sawyer said. "A lot of it is the margin. When the margin is that close, you have to go back and decide who was at fault." Cody's Wish won by a nose, the smallest amount possible.

Once they decided on an inquiry, Jauregui informed Mirahmadi, and Baker called down to the winner's circle to let them know which jockeys they wanted to speak to, although it was obvious Prat and Alvarado were the only two they needed. Baker got the jockeys' side of the story, which Sawyer said had value, because there were times they'd point out something the stewards missed, and they could go back and look at the replay again. Sawyer and Jauregui were watching the replay on two sixty-inch TVs, both with the capability of showing four angles at the same time. NFL RedZone fans know this as the quad-box.

Was Cody's Wish to blame for contact that cost National Treasure a placing? As the stewards deliberated, the majority of the crowd of 66,247 was now aware of what was going on, and, as the minutes passed, some became restless.

Cheers of "Leave him up" could be heard cascading from the grandstand, while in the winner's circle Godolphin's Dan Pride said to no one in particular, "They'll burn this place down if they take him [Cody's Wish] down."

Bill Mott told NBC's Kenny Rice that the contact was mutual and he didn't think it changed the outcome of the race. Baffert never left his seat. Even though there was a chance his horse would be declared the winner, he felt as if he were in a no-win situation. Sure, he would love to add another Breeders' Cup to his résumé, but not at the expense of this horse, this boy, and this story, and under these circumstances.

"I understood why they would take a look at it, because it was so close," he said, "but I have always felt that if it's a fifty-fifty call, they should leave the winner up. Both horses ran a winning race, but there are some things bigger than even winning. There was a part of me that felt we just got beat. We had the whole length of the stretch to win the race and he was the better horse. I would have felt horrible if they had taken that horse down."

The waiting was torture.

Leslie knew Cody would be crestfallen if this ultimate win were taken away, so she started to prepare herself mentally, God forbid it come to pass. Cody was already trying to process that there would be no more Cody's Wish races to watch, but at least he was going out a winner. Explaining a loss by disqualification was something she and Kelly were not remotely ready to do.

If Alvarado felt the weight of the earth on his shoulders before the race, now you could throw in the other seven planets in the solar system. Invariably when a horse is disqualified, the jockey gets the blame. He should have straightened him out, he should have gone to the other hand with the crop, he should have used the reins more effectively . . . the list goes on.

The video shows the crop never leaving Alvarado's left hand down the stretch, indicating he was encouraging Cody's Wish to move away from National Treasure. Prat was also using his left hand and once the two horses came together, Alvarado had no room to switch. There was a point in the final yards when Prat's right elbow made contact with Alvarado.

None of that made Alvarado feel better as he was overcome with negative thoughts. If Cody's Wish were disqualified, the horse might not be the only one headed for retirement.

"I felt like my world was crashing down on me," he said. "I kept thinking, 'If this horse gets taken down, I might just quit.' That would just ruin me. I'll never be able to recover from winning the Breeders' Cup and getting taken down."

That would have been the cruelest of ironies for Alvarado, who credits Cody's Wish with resurrecting his career.

"This horse turned everything around for me," he said. "He pulled me back in, put me right at the top."

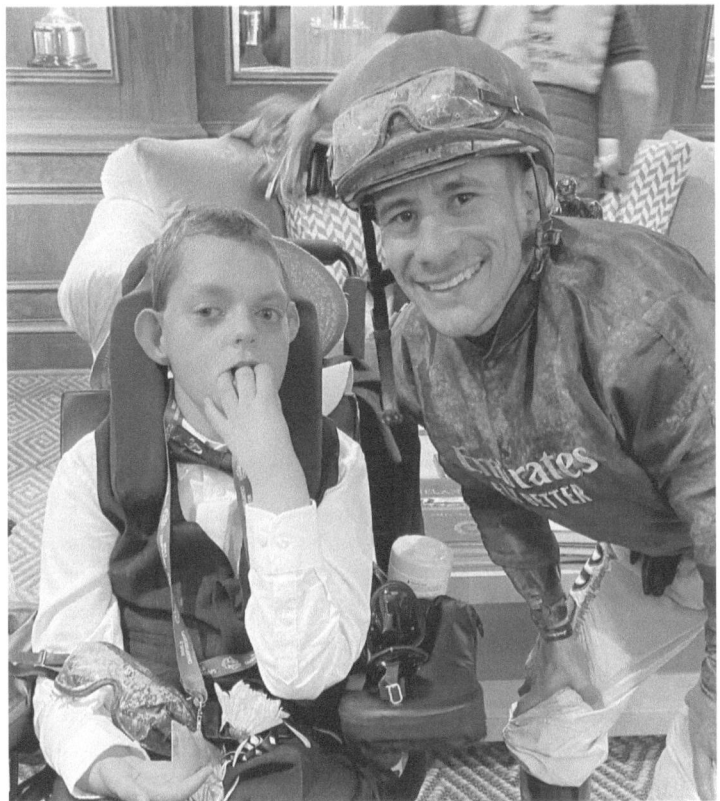

Junior Alvarado felt heavy pressure not to let Cody down in Cody's Wish's last career race. DORMAN FAMILY.

Did Cody's Wish save his career?

"Yes," he said.

And now that career could be ruined by a decision of the stewards. Somehow, that didn't seem fair.

Fifteen months after seriously contemplating retirement, Alvarado stood in the Santa Anita winner's circle, at the pinnacle of his career, thanks to a special horse and a special boy. Yet even in the brilliant California sunshine, he could again see darkness, and the longer it took for the stewards to make their ruling, it was closing in on him with the speed of Cody's Wish storming down the stretch.

Finally, the verdict . . .

"NO CHANGE."

All it took was Mirahmadi saying those two words to let everyone know the storybook ending was back. The five minutes the stewards took

A capacity crowd filled the Santa Anita winner's circle. BILL DENVER/ECLIPSE SPORTSWIRE/BREEDERS' CUP.

to make the decision seemed like five hours, but all's well that ends well. The celebration was back on, with more than fifty people cramming into the official win photo, including a handful of noncredentialed crashers who had met the Dormans at the Whitney Eve barbecue in Saratoga and felt such a strong connection they were determined to be part of this seminal moment.

Sawyer saw the contact between Cody's Wish and National Treasure as mutual and felt it did not affect the outcome. "When both contribute, it's an easier decision," she said.

All three stewards voted to leave the order of finish unchanged.

The announcement was met with a thunderous roar from the Santa Anita crowd, something Sawyer found odd.

"I thought, 'Why is it so loud?'" she said. "Usually we get booed when we make a decision."

She was told the crowd was so happy because Cody's Wish had stayed up, which prompted an incredible admission.

"I didn't even realize it was Cody's Wish," she said a few weeks after the race. "I know it sounds bizarre, but we had other things going on up there and it's the Breeders' Cup and I don't study it ahead of time, so I know it's probably not believable, but that's exactly what happened for me."

Whether the lead steward should have been aware of the protagonists in the inquiry drama is up for debate, but Sawyer swears she was not. When she realized it was Cody's Wish who remained the winner, "it made me feel really good," she said. "The story does put tears in your eyes. The whole story is very heartwarming."

And what if they had disqualified Cody's Wish?

"We probably wouldn't be talking," she said.

Even though this was the Breeders' Cup, where races are extremely difficult to win, with a $350,000 difference in prize money between first and second place, Baffert had zero complaint with the final result.

"We didn't deserve to be put up. If we were, we wouldn't have felt good," he said. "I mean, I was following Cody's Wish. We've seen horses that everybody talks about and starts following. Just like Zenyatta [19-for-20 lifetime] had a following. Rachel Alexandra [2009 Horse of the Year] had a following. You always made sure you watched those horses run, like Silver Charm [Baffert's 1997 Kentucky Derby and Preakness winner]. Everybody wanted to watch him run because he was the same way. He would will himself to win the race. He just found a way. And Cody's Wish found a way to win."

Prat had a similar feeling.

"I was fully aware of the story, and I think it's honestly a great story," he said one day in the paddock at Keeneland. "And for him to win the last race. . . . As time goes by, I would feel very bad if they would have put me up. In the moment, obviously I do my job and I defend the connections that I'm riding for. But for sure I think it was the right thing to do."

Alvarado could start breathing again.

"My soul just came back to my body," he said. "From the worst feeling to the best feeling ever. It was unbelievable."

Eighty-three years after Red Pollard—a half-blind jockey coming back from a broken leg—rode Seabiscuit to a redemptive victory in the Santa Anita Handicap, Junior Alvarado found his own vindication in the same winner's circle. Within eighteen months, he would win his first Kentucky Derby and Belmont Stakes, riding Godolphin-owned and Mott-trained Sovereignty to victory in two of the three legs of the 2025 Triple Crown.

Euphoria wasn't the only emotion Alvarado felt when "Official" lit up on the tote board.

"Normally, when we ride good horses, we want them to keep running and winning, and we keep making money, but I was so relieved that was the last race," he said. "To be honest, the pressure was very overwhelming. It was different. I don't care what anyone says, I have to be in the top five riders in stakes races. I rarely make a mistake. I can ride any horse and get the best from them. But that was it for me. I never felt pressure like that with any other horse. As much as I love this, it's going to eat me alive. It was something I never, ever felt before."

To the victor go the flowers. DORMAN FAMILY.

Kelly Dorman told reporters what this majestic racehorse had done for his son.

"That horse probably saved Cody's life," he said. "And I know he and that horse have made a lot of lives better."

Seventeen years after a doctor predicted Cody wouldn't live to see his second birthday, this might have been his best day ever.

17

Going Home

For Cody's Wish and Cody Dorman, November 5, 2023, was the first day of the rest of their lives.

The equine Cody flew from California to Cincinnati and then took a van to Lexington to prepare for his second career as a stallion at Jonabell Farm.

He joined a stallion roster led by Medaglia d'Oro, who ran second in the Belmont Stakes and two Breeders' Cup Classics; Nyquist, the 2016 Kentucky Derby winner; and Essential Quality, who won the Belmont the day after Cody's Wish's trouble-filled debut in 2021.

Godolphin waited until after the Breeders' Cup to set Cody's Wish's stallion fee, announced at $75,000 November 5. That was only $10,000 less than Nyquist, the highest-priced Darley stallion at the time (his fee was up to $175,000 in 2025). It was aggressive, but between the horse's regal pedigree, back-to-back Breeders' Cup wins, and captivating story, the team was confident Cody's Wish would be in demand as a freshman sire.

The human Cody and his family had an early wake-up call to fly from LA to Lexington, with a connection in Atlanta. After an exhilarating and exhausting week, they hit a wall Saturday night, opting for room service over another restaurant.

When they checked in for their 7 a.m. flight, they got some good news: Delta Flight 780 had two open seats in the Comfort+ section, just behind first class, and they were offered to the Dormans. It would be much easier to get Cody on and off the plane, so Leslie and Cody took those seats while Kelly and Kylie headed back to the main cabin.

Cody was a first-on, last-off airline passenger. Not long after Leslie had him settled into his seat, one of the flight attendants identified herself as a former nurse and told her if they needed anything during the flight, just ask for her. "Good to know," Leslie thought, though not expecting to have to take her up on the offer.

Sitting in the middle seat, Cody was fidgety during the flight, so Leslie tried to make sure he was not bothering the man in the window seat next to him. She didn't take a drink or snack the first time the flight attendants came around.

Cody seemed fine, just overtired from a draining week. They had him checked out by a doctor before traveling to California, and everything looked good. He had recently received a clean bill of health from his longtime cardiologist, Dr. Russel Hirsch at Cincinnati Children's. He had a cough in the hotel Friday night, but Leslie suctioned him—nothing out of the ordinary—and he fell asleep.

There was less than an hour left in the flight when another round of snacks was offered, and this time Leslie accepted. As she sipped on her soft drink, Cody laid his head on her shoulder and went to sleep.

Taking care of Cody was the ultimate team game, but Kelly has no doubt about the captain.

"Ninety-five percent her and five percent me," he said, and while that is an exaggeration, you get the point.

Cody appreciated everything his parents did for him, though he resented that his condition forced him to be completely dependent. As his eighteenth birthday approached and his teachers started talking about jobs he might be able to take on at some point, he told them he would never be able to work, because "I can't go anywhere without my momma."

As the plane was landing at Hartsfield-Jackson Atlanta International Airport, Leslie tried to wake Cody. She noticed his hands were blue, and when she felt them, they were cold—not unusual because Cody had Raynaud's disease, in which smaller arteries narrow, limiting blood flow to the skin.

Leslie started rubbing Cody's hands to get the blood flowing, and she lifted his head off her shoulder. When she got a look at him, the situation suddenly stopped being routine. Something was wrong. Very wrong.

By now the plane was at the gate and most of the other passengers were headed to their next destination. Leslie yelled for a flight attendant, and when one arrived, she asked for the former nurse. When that attendant got to their row and caught a glimpse of Cody, she immediately reached for oxygen. She told Leslie she could barely feel a pulse, but Cody always had a weak pulse, so that didn't shock his mother.

As Kelly and Kylie gathered their carry-ons and started heading up the aisle, Kelly noticed there was some commotion around Leslie's row and saw the flight attendant pull down the oxygen mask. He didn't panic, though once he reached the row behind Leslie and Cody, he observed that his wife seemed more worried than usual as a grizzled caregiver.

Kelly was thinking it could be a seizure, and even though being on an airplane was far from ideal, they had medications they could give him. As the flight attendant started to lay Cody flat across the seats, Kelly was concerned about his fragile neck being hurt, so he came around to hold his head. That's when he looked down and saw his son's face for the first time since the ordeal began.

"We revived him two or three times when he was younger," Kelly said. "And I always remember looking in his eyes. I didn't panic even then. Somehow, you just go to another place because you know you got a job to do. If you don't do it, you're going to lose him. And all those times and situations, I never did panic, but when I looked at his face this time, it was something different, something I had not seen before. It was like looking in someone's eyes and they're not there anymore."

Kelly started tapping Cody on the cheek. No response. The flight attendant was doing chest compressions, but Cody's facial expression remained unchanged. His eyes did not blink. The paramedics arrived and took over CPR, laying Cody on the floor of the plane. Kelly held his legs and urged him to be the fighter he had been for almost eighteen years.

"Come on, Bubby, just fight it one more time like you always have," Kelly pleaded with his son, still thinking—or maybe by this point hoping—that it could be a severe seizure.

The paramedics used an automated external defibrillator to shock Cody's heart several times. He was still unresponsive, and they needed to get him to the hospital. They put him on a stretcher and one of the medics straddled him, one knee on either side of his waist, continuing chest compressions as they wheeled him up the jet bridge.

Dan Pride and his wife, Beth, sat three rows in front of Leslie and Cody on the flight. They had deplaned, along with Michael Banahan and his wife, Kathryn, and headed for the gate for the flight to Lexington, unaware of the traumatic scene. Pride had already arrived at the other concourse and texted Kelly a few photos from Saturday that he found on social media. He got a sobering response.

"Cody's in trouble. Paramedics on the way."

Pride rushed back to the gate where the Delta flight had landed, arriving in time to see the paramedics working on Cody in the jet bridge. Kylie was also watching this situation unfold, so he quickly got her away from the door, giving her a hug and trying to reassure her.

"She was in shock," Pride said. "She knew there was a major problem."

After a few minutes, the stretcher was wheeled through the gate area, heading for the ambulance. They needed to go a few gates away to use an elevator to access the tarmac below, where the ambulance was waiting. Dan, Kelly, Leslie, and Kylie took the stairs, Pride reminding Leslie to keep breathing.

They couldn't all fit in the ambulance headed for Children's Healthcare of Atlanta Hughes Spalding Hospital, so Kelly, Leslie, and Kylie were driven in an SUV. Pride said he would meet them there, after making sure their carry-on luggage from the flight was secure. He knew he didn't have much time, so he sought out a Delta employee to help. He found Andre Hill and explained the situation.

"He said he would take care of it and that's what he did," Pride said. "He was a star."

Pride got an Uber and headed for the hospital. On the way he called Keith Mason, a partner in West Paces Racing, an Atlanta-based group that won the 2024 Belmont Stakes with Dornoch. Mason knew an administrator at Hughes Spalding, and he got word to the hospital that Cody was on the way.

There was heavy traffic and the SUV got separated from the ambulance, which arrived first. When the Dormans got to the hospital, Kelly made a dash for the emergency room and was directed to where Cody was being treated. He was jolted by what he saw.

More than a dozen doctors and nurses were feverishly working on Cody. Kelly turned to intercept Leslie and Kylie to ensure that his daughter did not see something she might never be able to erase from her memory. One of the nurses took Kylie away while Kelly and Leslie watched the final stages of a valiant medical effort befitting the nearly eighteen-year battle waged by the boy they were trying to save.

"You always hold on to that shred of hope," Kelly said. "He found a way out of so many things. As long as there's that little flicker of light, he had a chance of coming back."

Cody arrived at the hospital at 2:30 p.m. Eastern time, exactly twenty-four hours after Cody's Wish entered the starting gate at Santa Anita for his final race, a win that put an exclamation point on a championship career. Now Cody, too, had finished his race.

"Time of death: three fifteen," one of the doctors said. It was just like on TV, but for the Dormans this horror show was very real.

Kelly approached the table holding his son's lifeless body. He put his arms around Cody's head and cried like never before. Leslie was by his side, also overwhelmed with a sadness that cuts through your heart in the express lane to your soul.

Kelly and Leslie had lived 6,531 days knowing this moment could come at any time, so they could never be considered fully unprepared. But if they ever needed a reason to simply appreciate being parents and not worry, the euphoria of another Breeders' Cup win that capped a glorious period of Cody living his best life certainly provided one.

After the initial shock wore off, the parents faced an impossible task, for which Kelly had no idea where he would find the strength.

He went to an adjacent room where Kylie was waiting. The nurses had given her a coloring book and crayons to try to provide a dose of normalcy on this nightmare of a day. Kelly sat on a coffee table across from Kylie and Leslie. He knew what he had to say, but the words were nowhere to be found.

A few minutes after hearing a doctor pronounce his son dead, Kelly broke the news to Cody's sister.

"That was the hardest thing I've ever done in my life," he said. "I couldn't get it out. It took every fiber in me to tell her that Bubby was gone."

Kelly, Leslie, and Kylie held each other tight. As they cried and cried and cried some more, Kelly noticed something on the wall. There were two framed drawings, done in crayon. Both were of horses.

"It was like he was telling us, 'I'm all right.' We actually laughed a little bit," Kelly said. "Bubby was telling us he's OK."

Pride arrived at the hospital, and it was as if he were sent by Cody to make sure his parents and sister would be OK. Kelly said something he has repeated multiple times since.

"We were never afraid of Cody dying," Kelly told Pride. "We were only afraid of him not living."

They had nothing to fear in that regard. Their commitment to providing their son with the best existence possible under the most challenging circumstances, combined with Cody's zest for life that had been rejuvenated by his equine best friend, ensured that Cody did indeed live a happy and fulfilling life.

Was he aware that his life was in its final stage as he spent those four days at Santa Anita? Was Cody's last wish to see his friend go out on top?

Those questions can never be answered, but his parents quickly resolved themselves to the idea that their son wasn't going anywhere until his horse ran his last race. After that, all bets were off.

"Waking us up to thank us for taking him out there, I feel like he wasn't only thanking us," Leslie said a few weeks after Cody died. "He was telling us that he was done. He put in his work and it was time to go."

As the Dormans tried to figure out what to do next, they were greeted by a nurse. Word had gotten out about Cody and Cody's Wish, and she had googled the story.

"As nurses, we do our best to keep emotion out of it," the ER nurse told Kelly. "All of us here have looked up the story and we can't think of a child who made such an impact in this hospital as Cody has in the short time he's been here."

While Kelly and Leslie met with the medical examiner and answered some questions, Pride tried to arrange a flight back to Lexington. He started with Delta, but the more he thought about it, the more he realized that even if there were seats available, that wouldn't be a good idea.

Any flight headed to Lexington the day after the Breeders' Cup would be filled with people returning home from the event. Pride knew the sight of three Dormans without Cody would lead to questions they were in no way ready to answer. He called Sentient Jet, a sponsor of horse racing, and arranged for a private flight out of Gwinnett County, around forty miles away.

A master logistician (a skill he frequently applied as the chief operating officer of Godolphin USA), Pride was the perfect person to be the Dormans' travel agent and guardian angel.

"Dan Pride was a godsend to us that night," Kelly said. "He took care of every single detail. There was nothing that we had to worry about other than some paperwork at the hospital. I wasn't going to leave without Cody. I was going to ride back with him, but by state law you can't cross state lines with a body that's not been prepared. So he had to go to a funeral home there."

As they eventually flew back to Lexington, Kelly couldn't help but consider the irony of having never been on any airplane until a year ago, and now he was on this luxurious private jet.

"Look where Bubby has taken us now," he said to his wife and daughter.

In their darkest hour, they were able to chuckle.

In Garden City, New York, Junior Alvarado got a call from his agent around 8:30 p.m.

"Junior," Mike Sellitto said, "I've got some bad news."

Alvarado thought something bad might have happened to Sellitto or someone in his family. His mind started racing, trying to fathom what his agent would say next. Cody dying was not among the scenarios he envisioned.

"Are you sure, Mike?" Alvarado asked. "Are you sure?"

He was sure.

Kelly Alvarado had seen her husband cry only once or twice in their fifteen years together, so when he got off the phone and had a tear in his eye, she asked him what was wrong. Like Kelly Dorman in Atlanta hours earlier, Alvarado struggled to get the words out. When he did, his wife crumpled to the floor.

"I had to pull myself together for her and pick her up," Alvarado said. "We sat on the couch and she bawled her eyes out. I was still trying to figure out how this was possible."

When the jet landed in Lexington, the Dormans' luggage, carry-ons, and Cody's wheelchair were waiting for them. They got in Kelly's truck and headed home to Richmond. The next day, funeral director Jeff Jessie arranged for Cody's body to be transported to Columbia, where his wake and funeral would be held at the end of the week.

On Thursday, November 9, at 3trees Church in Russell Springs, Kentucky, around thirteen miles east of Columbia, people from all corners of Cody Dorman's world—horse racing, Future Farmers of America, motorcycle and car clubs, bass fishing, teachers, doctors—approached an open casket covered with the garland of flowers draped across Cody's Wish five days earlier, the saddlecloth he had worn in the Forego, a set of Alvarado's goggles, some fishing gear, and photos.

In the coffin lay the peaceful-looking body of Cody Layne Dorman, wearing his blue suit, bow tie, and matching scally cap. Cody had in his hands a $2 win ticket on Cody's Wish from the Breeders' Cup Dirt Mile, worth $3.60, but a priceless item that would go with Cody to his final resting place.

For more than six hours on Thursday and three hours on Friday morning, Kelly and Leslie stood in front of their son's casket and accepted the sympathy of hundreds, though there were plenty of times when they did the consoling. Leslie's nephews, Dylan and Colton Feese, doted on their cousin, Kylie.

One of the mourners Friday was the night watchman from Gainesway Farm in Lexington, where the leading stallion is Tapit, the sire of Dance Card, Cody's Wish's mother. He worked his overnight shift and then drove an hour and forty-five minutes to pay his respects to the Dormans, giving them a ball of hair he had clipped from Tapit's mane the night before.

At 10:59 a.m. on November 10, Kelly and Leslie embraced as they shared a final moment with their son before the funeral service began,

Cody was laid to rest on November 10, 2023, at Haven Hill Cemetery in Columbia, Kentucky. PAUL HALLORAN.

Brother Paul Patton and Brother Drew Hayes presiding. The horse racing world was well represented in the congregation of about 150—Pride, Banahan, Danny Mulvihill, Mary Bourne, and others from Godolphin; Breeders' Cup CEO Drew Fleming; Amy Zimmerman from NBC and Santa Anita; Bill Mott; his assistant, Penny Gardiner; and Mike Sellitto, Alvarado's agent.

Faith Hacker of Make-A-Wish spoke, followed by Mulvihill, who had picked the right foal to introduce to Cody on that fateful afternoon in 2018. In his eulogy, Brother Patton said that as hard as this loss was to accept, all should genuinely feel good for Cody, now unencumbered by the shackles of Wolf-Hirschhorn syndrome and all of his physical ailments.

"Cody is home in the presence of God," he said. "He has no limitations—physical or emotional. Love allowed Cody to thrive in ways that doctors might not have expected."

Brother Patton referenced Psalm 23:4 and said, "Death is a journey, not a destination."

The last stop on Cody's earthly journey was Haven Hill Cemetery in Columbia, where Steve Buttleman stood on a hillside under a sky that had transitioned from morning rain to afternoon sunshine. Buttleman, the

Cody's gravestone was designed by his father. DORMAN FAMILY.

bugler at Churchill Downs and Keeneland, who had met the Dormans at the 2022 Breeders' Cup, was dressed in his race-day uniform: black hat, red jacket, white pants, shiny black boots.

As Cody's casket was lifted out of the hearse, Buttleman raised a B-flat herald trumpet to his lips and played "Call to Post," a thirty-four-note ditty that signals it is time to bring horses to the track. On this day, it served as melancholy background music as six pallbearers carried a coffin to a grave prepared for a seventeen-year-old boy.

With dozens of graveside mourners already struggling to hold it together, Buttleman made that practically impossible when he segued into "My Old Kentucky Home," the official state song of Kentucky and a staple at the Kentucky Derby. When the University of Louisville band plays Stephen Foster's anthem as the horses enter the racetrack on the first Saturday in May, it's not uncommon for fans to sob.

> Weep no more my lady, oh! Weep no more today!
> We will sing one song for the old Kentucky home
> For the old Kentucky home far away.

It might have been easier to beat Cody's Wish around a racetrack than hold back tears. It was a moment filled with raw emotion, the climax of the journey of a boy and the racehorse who saved his life and became his best friend.

Both went out on top.

18

Celebration of Lives

When Cody got his communication tablet just before Christmas in 2017, one of the first times he used it was when he asked his mother to bring him to the window so he could watch it snow.

"Cody loved the snow," Kelly Dorman said, standing outside the stallion barn at Jonabell Farm on December 18, 2023, a light snow falling as if sent by his son.

Around fifty of the Dormans' family and friends joined them to commemorate Cody's eighteenth birthday, forty-three days after he died on the way home from the Breeders' Cup. It was part birthday party, part celebration of life—and all special.

Graham "Jimmy" Lovatt brought Cody's Wish—the newest member of Darley's All-Star stallion lineup—outside, where the wind howled and the snow intensified, prompting someone to crack, "OK, Cody, we get it. Enough with the snow already."

Six weeks after ending his career with a second consecutive win in the Breeders' Cup Dirt Mile, Cody's Wish looked the picture of health. Had he been standing in the paddock before a Grade 1 race, you'd have expected the experts to deem him the most likely winner.

"He's settled in nicely," said Lovatt, the stallion manager at Jonabell. "He's a happy boy."

The champion racehorse turned stallion looked especially pleased when Kylie fed him an oversized cupcake. Happy birthday to you, too, Cody's Wish.

Lovatt said Cody's Wish was brought to the breeding shed for a test run and he passed with flying colors.

Cody's Wish came out to meet guests gathered on what would have been Cody's eighteenth birthday, as the snow fell at Jonabell Farm. PAUL HALLORAN.

"He's such a pleasure to work with. He's a true professional in the breeding shed already. We had an open house with more than one thousand visitors. His book is full."

Breeding season began, appropriately, on February 14. Cody's Wish covered 165 mares, getting 151 in foal: a 91.5 percent success rate, the best of all the Darley stallions in 2024 and as good as any Godolphin sire ever with that many mares.

"He's special in every way," Dan Pride said.

One of the attendees at the birthday celebration was renowned sculptor and artist Jocelyn Russell, whose life-size statue of Secretariat had been on display throughout the year at the major races, including all three Triple Crown events and the Whitney at Saratoga, where she met the Dormans.

Russell wasn't at Jonabell just for the birthday cake; she was taking detailed measurements of Cody's Wish for a future masterpiece.

There was another statue Godolphin had in mind: the trophy for the Horse of the Year, to be presented at the Eclipse Awards at the Breakers in Palm Beach, Florida, in January. The Dormans already had an Eclipse in their home, after Jack Felling gave Cody the one he and NBC had won for the segment that ran on the 2022 Breeders' Cup broadcast. Cody's Wish was considered the favorite for Horse of the Year, but the winner is not revealed until the night of the ceremony, so there were no guarantees.

Godolphin was a finalist for top owner and breeder, and had horses in other categories, so team members were going to Palm Beach one way or another. Figuring there was a good chance Cody's Wish would be named Horse of the Year, they invited the Dormans, hoping they would be open to traveling less than three months after the ill-fated trip home from California.

The family accepted the invite, and their itinerary had them flying from Lexington to Palm Beach—with a stop in Atlanta. That was a bit unnerving, considering what had transpired November 5, and as the plane descended, Leslie and Kylie were visibly upset.

Fortunately, they had a long enough layover to get something to eat and gather themselves. As they settled in on Delta Flight 1190 from ATL to PBI, a flight attendant stopped at their row. "I'm so glad to see you traveling again," she told them.

It didn't register immediately, but then they figured it out: She had been on their flight from Los Angeles to Atlanta. What were the chances?

"It was emotional," Kelly said. "She's a friend of the flight attendant who worked on Cody. We thanked her for everything they did. It goes to show you, these aren't just people pushing a cart and giving you a Diet Coke and a bag of chips."

At the Eclipse Awards ceremony, by the time they got to Horse of the Year, Godolphin had already collected four trophies: outstanding owner, outstanding breeder, three-year-old filly (Pretty Mischievous), and older dirt male (Cody's Wish). Bill Mott was named top trainer, and he had Just F Y I win for two-year-old filly and Elite Power as male sprinter.

It was already a memorable night for the team in royal blue, but for all its success, Godolphin had never campaigned a Horse of the Year. That was the coveted award.

National Thoroughbred Racing Association president and CEO Tom Rooney had the honor of presenting Horse of the Year. When it came time to make the announcement, he enlisted a special assistant.

"I'd like to get some help up here, if I could, to announce Horse of the Year," he said. "Kylie Dorman, could you come up here and help me do Horse of the Year."

Rooney managed to simultaneously remove the suspense and intensify the drama.

Wearing a black dress and a big smile, Kylie got up from her seat in front of the stage. She had been told she would have some role in the awards ceremony but didn't know it would be this. She took the envelope from Rooney and broke the seal. As she removed the card from the envelope, Rooney handed her the microphone.

"Cody's Wish," she said, the ballroom erupting in applause.

At some point in the days leading up to the Eclipse Awards, Pride told Kelly that if Cody's Wish won Horse of the Year, Kelly would be accepting the award on behalf of Godolphin. Kelly reminded Pride that Godolphin had been waiting more than twenty years to win this particular award. Wouldn't it be better if Pride or Michael Banahan accepted?

As they had been doing for more than five years since Cody and his family showed up at Gainsborough Farm, the Godolphin team put the Dormans first. There was no argument: Kelly would accept the award.

"Oh, man, I don't know if I've got the words," he started, becoming emotional when a picture of Cody and Cody's Wish from their first meeting was projected onto a screen. "I never would have dreamed five years ago that I would be standing right here doing this. The wonderful people we've met. You guys just blow me away, because I know you put your heart in these horses. . . . That horse, he put his heart into us."

The day after the ceremony, before heading to the airport, Kelly, Leslie, and Kylie stopped to see the ocean for the first time. Kylie told her parents she wanted to say a prayer for Cody. She also had something she wanted to give him.

Holding a flower from the Eclipse Awards, Kylie stepped into the ocean and, with the tide receding, waded into water barely above her ankles. She tossed the flower underhanded into the sea and then watched as it was engulfed by a wave.

Confident her gift was on the way to her beloved Bubby, Kylie returned to shore and a hug from Leslie, whose embrace enveloped both of her children—the one in her arms and the one waiting for that flower.

Epilogue

JOCELYN RUSSELL WAS AMONG THE 150,335 PEOPLE AT CHURCHILL DOWNS on Kentucky Derby Day 2023. She was there with the life-size bronze statue of Secretariat that she sculpted to coincide with the fiftieth anniversary of America's best racehorse winning the Triple Crown.

That was the first time Russell was exposed to the story of Cody and Cody's Wish, who ran in the Churchill Downs Stakes, two races before the Derby. Three months later, when she took Secretariat to Saratoga on the weekend of the National Museum of Racing Hall of Fame induction and the Whitney Stakes, she met Cody and his family.

As they exchanged pleasantries, Russell couldn't help but notice how much attention her dog, Alis Margaret, an Australian Shepherd, was paying to Cody.

"My dog fell in love with Cody and tried to crawl up on his lap," Russell said. "She didn't like young people, and she didn't like wheelchairs or strollers, but she was very enamored with Cody. She wanted to get as close as she possibly could to him. I thought that was intriguing because it was very similar to what the horse had been described as doing."

Russell was fully attuned to the story of the magical bond between the boy and the horse when she learned of Cody's death on November 5. She called her friend Robin Hutton, whose book on war horse Sergeant Reckless had served as the inspiration for another Russell masterpiece.

"I told Robin we have to do something as a tribute to that bond," Russell said.

So there she was on December 18 at Jonabell Farm when Cody's family and friends gathered on what would have been his eighteenth birthday. As others enjoyed some face time with the big horse and Kylie was feeding him a birthday cupcake, Russell was taking detailed measurements of his massive body.

A Colorado native, Russell started working for a veterinarian when she was twelve. Though she never went to vet tech school, she got a hands-on education that rivaled anything she could have learned in a classroom. She and her first husband worked for seventeen years on the cattle ranch they owned. She eventually moved to Washington State, where she lives with her current husband, Michael Dubail.

Russell began sculpting in 1992. Her first animal statue was a large elk. Sergeant Reckless, a decorated war horse who served with the Marines in the Korean War, was her third horse and the first work to put her in the national spotlight.

After getting approval from Godolphin to sculpt Cody's Wish, it was time to get to work, starting with taking photos and measurements at Jonabell Farm on Cody's birthday. She made a twelve-inch version out of clay, taking that to Jonabell a few times to compare with the real thing and then make adjustments. She then built a life-size version out of foam, which was eventually covered with a layer of clay, incorporating painstaking detail in each version.

"Nobody does the research like she does," said Hutton, who coordinated the fundraising for the Cody's Wish statue through Angels Without Wings, a nonprofit she founded that helps the poor and honors people who support animals that are in need, as well as animals that have served the country.

Once Russell finished the life-size clay version, she loaded it onto a truck for a sixteen-hour drive to her foundry in Utah. After she completed the final details, the 660-pound statue was cast in bronze and prepped for the seventeen-hundred-mile drive to Lexington, Kentucky.

When she was in the conceptual stage, Russell considered including a statue of Cody with Cody's Wish, but she ultimately decided to portray the horse as he looked when lowering his head to Cody's level. Her decision to leave the space below the horse's head open has both an intangible and a practical effect, inviting visitors to visualize their own image of Cody while also providing an opportunity for others, including those in wheelchairs, to occupy the same area and touch the horse's head.

"I think this is more of an interpretative experience and it makes it available to everybody," Russell said. "I love that he has his head lowered as he did when he was interacting with Cody. We wanted to offer Cody's space to others, allowing them to share his bond with Cody's Wish."

Instead of putting Cody in front of the horse, a few feet away there is a granite stone with the iconic image of the best friends—one that the

Kelly, Kylie, and Leslie Dorman were all smiles when they got a look at Jocelyn Russell's statue of Cody's Wish. BOBBY SHIFLET/FRAMES ON MAIN GALLERY.

bronzed Cody's Wish will perpetually gaze at. Another stone is engraved with a summary of the bond between the two. The two monuments are part of a circular installation that was conceived by Hutton—with plenty of input from the Dormans.

The U-Haul transporting the Cody's Wish statue arrived in Kentucky on September 29—twelve days before the formal dedication and unveiling at Kentucky Horse Park, a magnificent, state-owned, twelve-hundred-acre expanse. The park, which boasts of being "the world's only park dedicated to man's relationship with the horse," is home to forty statues—including Secretariat, the legendary Man o' War, two-time Horse of the Year Cigar, and thirty-nine-time winner John Henry—but Cody's Wish is the only one of a living horse, according to Lee Carter, executive director of the horse park.

"The whole story is so compelling," Russell said. "Every day I pinched myself that we were on such an amazing ride. I was very honored to be the artist working on this project."

On October 11, 2025—seven years to the day after Cody first met the horse who would become his best friend—more than five hundred people

Robin Hutton addresses the huge crowd that came to the statue dedication at the Kentucky Horse Park on October 11, 2025. BOBBY SHIFLET/FRAMES ON MAIN GALLERY.

gathered for the dedication ceremony. The crowd included people from all walks of Cody's life: horse racing, fishing, motorcycles, car clubs, and a multitude of friends and family. The Dormans were overwhelmed with the outpouring of love and support, although by that point they could have reasonably expected it.

"If you build it, they will come," Kelly Dorman said. "This is really incredible. I look throughout this crowd and I see friends I've had all my life, my family, people I've worked with in the past, work with now. Through all the friends that we've had, we have felt the hand of support on our back from the day Cody was born."

The ceremony began with bugler Steve Buttleman playing "Call to Post" and "My Old Kentucky Home," just as he did when Cody's casket was being carried to his grave. During the playing of the Kacey Musgraves song "Rainbow"—described by the singer as a message of hope for anyone facing adversity—Kylie placed her head on her father's shoulder and sobbed. She was not alone in that emotional outpouring.

For the occasion, Nashville singer/songwriter Bri Fletcher, who appeared on *The Voice*, composed an original song that opens with "The world didn't deal you the easiest cards, but you handled it with a graceful heart." The chorus perfectly captures Cody's journey with Cody's Wish:

Epilogue

Two souls aligning
was perfect timing,
said the most even in the silence.
Gave you something to cheer for
at the end of a rainstorm
you finally got to win
racing to live life to the fullest.
Thank God for Cody's Wish.

In a deeply emotional scene after the unveiling, the first person to enter the space under the bronze statue of Cody's Wish was Carson Jost, whom Cody met at the 2023 Breeders' Cup and who also suffers from Wolf-Hirschhorn syndrome. Carson, who is thirty-three, had traveled from Washington State with his parents, Wade and Kim, to be a part of the Dormans' special day.

More tissues, anyone?

The last words of the speaking program belonged to Cody. Leslie carried his tablet to the podium and handed it to Kelly, who had talked about

Carson Jost, whom Cody met at the 2023 Breeders' Cup, was the first person to be photographed with the Cody's Wish statue after the formal unveiling. BOBBY SHIFLET/FRAMES ON MAIN GALLERY.

The Cody's Wish statue appears to be staring at the image of Cody and the horse — and in this case the reflection of Cody's parents and sister. BOBBY SHIFLET/FRAMES ON MAIN GALLERY.

Cody always wanting to interact with people one on one, even in a large group. Kelly touched the screen and out came Cody's voice:
 "Thank you."
 "Thank you."
 "Thank you."
 "Thank you."

Thank you, Cody, for bringing us on the ride of a lifetime.

Thank you, Cody. ARIEL BOYD PHOTOGRAPHY.

Acknowledgments

THE TRAVERS STAKES AT SARATOGA HAS ALWAYS BEEN A SPECIAL DAY FOR me, since the first one I attended in 1992, when New York–bred Thunder Rumble pulled off an upset that was popular with the hometown fans. I've been to around twenty Travers since, the last seven as a writer for *The Saratoga Special*. That's why I was there on August 27, 2022, when Epicenter, who had finished a hard-luck second in the Kentucky Derby, won the big race. Four hours before the Travers, Cody's Wish won the Forego Stakes, which started in motion the journey that led to this book.

I am obviously grateful for drawing the assignment to cover the Forego, but beyond that I'm honored to be part of the *Special* team. In more than forty years of writing, my work there has provided as much fulfillment and professional pride as anything I have done. Thanks to Tom Law, Sean Clancy, and especially Joe Clancy, as good an editor as I have worked with, who did a thorough edit of this book as I prepared to bring it to publishers.

When I began in earnest the process of searching for a publisher, after the draft was written, it was recommended to me that I try to gauge the enthusiasm of those I approached. (Honestly, I would have been happy with anything more than mild interest.) Brittany Stoner at Lyons Press responded to my first email in an hour—sixty-two minutes, to be exact—and she has been everything I could have hoped for in an editor and advocate for this book. She made it a seamless process for this first-time author, and every time I saw her edits or spoke to her, I felt better about the manuscript. She is Grade 1 all the way, as is assistant managing editor Patricia Stevenson.

There is a legion of others who have been enthusiastically supportive since I embarked on this project in early 2023, starting with the good people at Godolphin, including Michael Banahan, Mary Bourne,

Johnny Burke, Jim Cox, Graham "Jimmy" Lovatt, Danny Mulvihill, and Dan Pride. I went back to Danny and Dan many times throughout the process to ask questions and confirm facts and figures, and the response was always instantaneous. Jim Cox became an unknowing photo consultant late in the game, and he came through in spades. Dan, a walk-on football player at the University of Georgia, is the guy who gets things done. Always. Being an eyewitness to the compassion, respect, and love Team Godolphin has shown for the Dormans has been a privilege. They are simply the best.

The same can be said for Faith Hacker and Make-A-Wish, who can take credit for establishing the connection between Cody and Cody's Wish and welcoming the Dormans into the greater Make-A-Wish family. They are indeed doing God's work.

Junior Alvarado is a champion jockey but an even better human being. As Kelly Dorman has often said, he was the perfect third leg of the trifecta that included Cody and Cody's Wish. Getting to know Junior and his wonderful wife, Kelly, has been one of the highlights of this process, and I value their friendship.

Thanks to Bill Mott and his team—Kenny McCarthy, Penny Gardiner, Neil Poznansky, Erma Scott (perhaps the most beloved woman in racing), and Ana Urista Hernandez, Cody's Wish's faithful groom—for their masterful work with the horse and embracing a story that transcends any horse race.

I appreciate Larry Collmus, Ahmed Fareed, Jack Felling, and Tom Hammond of NBC taking the time to discuss how the story of Cody and Cody's Wish impacted so many who work for the network. I am sincerely grateful to Tom, a Hall of Fame broadcaster by any measure, for writing the foreword.

The Breeders' Cup plays a central role in this story, and I was fortunate that Claire Crosby, Drew Fleming, and Jim Gluckson supported my efforts.

Sandy Burgin gave me my first sportswriting job when I was a senior in college. He remains a good friend, and it was special to introduce him to the Dormans at the 2024 Breeders' Cup. I'm grateful to Tim Wilkin, as hardworking a turf writer as there is, for facilitating one of the key interviews.

Covering horse racing is a side job for me—OK, an obsession—but in my professional career I have worked for and with Ted Grant in one way or another for four decades. A BC guy taking a chance on a Holy Cross guy in 1985 has been a life-altering decision for me, and I appreciate Ted as a boss, coworker, and friend. I thank him for giving me the flexibility to take the time to work on this book.

Acknowledgments

When you're a rookie in any endeavor, you rely on the veterans. In my case, I had the great fortune of being able to call on authors Robin Hutton, Jennifer Kelly, Matt Miller, Stephen Panus, Roger Peach, Josh Pons, Beth Pride (Dan's better half), Dan Shaughnessy, and Kim Wickens for guidance, advice, referrals, you name it. I appreciate all of them. Special thanks to Beth for being a beta reader and Josh for the connection to Brittany and Lyons Press. And to Matt for his editorial and legal skills. He truly is a great partner in every respect.

Graphic designer Amanda Lunn of Grant Communications lent her considerable skills to the editing of photos. I appreciate her ongoing efforts to make me and the company look good.

Speaking of photos, I am sincerely grateful to the immensely talented Barbara Livingston of the Daily Racing Form for allowing me to use the cover image that perfectly illustrates the bond between a special boy and a champion horse. Thanks also to the photographers whose work appears in this book, including Ariel Boyd, Bill Denver, Mathea Kelley, Krystal Mitchell, Bobby Shiflet, and John Voorhees, as well as Scott Serio of Eclipse Sportswire.

I appreciate Dr. Robert Hopkin and Dr. Cameron Thomas, both of whom treated Cody for most of his life, for taking the time to shed light on the monumental struggle he and his family faced.

Prior to my first trip to see the Dormans in April 2023, I had never been to Kentucky. I'm not sure how I can call myself a true horse racing fan without going to Keeneland until I was almost sixty (gulp). That mistake has been rectified, and, God willing, I will always be a twice-a-year visitor to one of the world's greatest racetracks. I appreciate the hospitality of all the friendly faces and Green Jackets at Keeneland, especially Buff Bradley, Jim Goodman, Jim Navolio, Kevin O'Keeffe, and Misty Oatsvall, who makes the Green Room such a special oasis.

This book will be far from the last word on this special story. It has been gratifying to work with Jeff Celentano and Warren Ostergard as they prepare to bring it to the big screen. They and their talented team are committed to honoring Cody's memory while sharing his story with a worldwide audience, and it is a privilege to play a small part in those efforts.

Throughout researching this book—and where better to do that than the track?—I have encountered a plethora of touching moments. The meeting of Cody and Carson Jost on the backstretch at Santa Anita is near the top of the list, and I wish Carson and his parents, Wade and Kim, all the best. Like the Dormans, they were chosen for a mission that can be executed only by the elite among us.

I'm not sure I've ever seen so many grown men—and hardened horseplayers—as genuinely touched to meet someone as my crew was to meet Cody at our rental home in Saratoga Springs in 2023. From my yearly roommates—Jaime Herman, Dr. Jeff Morer, Bob Mullins, and Tom Sofish—to Howard Kravets, Matt Miller, Kyle Roscoe, Pete Visco, and the rest of the *HHH Racing Podcast* team, to longtime colleague and friend Rich Fahey and the Suffolk Downs Chelsea guys Eddie Rosa, Stuart Feinberg, and Jim "Buddha" Barbati, everyone was in some level of awe when Kelly Dorman wheeled Cody into the house. He was a rock star, and we were the groupies.

Speaking of Bob Mullins, he is on a list of loyal friends who have lived through this project with me, offering constant encouragement and unwavering support. That group includes Jim Girardi and Michael Germano, with whom I cumulatively share a century of friendship. Everyone should have people like that in their corner.

When Kelly and Leslie Dorman agreed to entrust me with their son's story, none of us could have anticipated it would take us to a place where the Dormans and the Hallorans consider each other family. For that, and the honor of telling that story, I am eternally grateful, as I am for having Kylie become one of my favorite people.

I am fully aware and sincerely appreciative of the role my family has played in this book, especially my wife, Julie, who watched me walk out the door headed for another writing session at Staples countless times without ever questioning it, even though it meant she would be flying solo with our adult daughter, Martha, whose profound autism presents its own set of challenges. Our other daughter, Kathryn, and her husband, Ben (thank you, Villanova), have been stalwarts in their support, and Kathryn's edit of the final manuscript proved invaluable.

Most of all, thank you to Cody Dorman, simply one of the toughest and most resilient human beings I've ever met, and Cody's Wish, whose excellence on the racetrack ensured that he would live up to his name.

Thanks for reading.

www.ingramcontent.com/pod-product-compliance
Ingram Content Group UK Ltd.
Pitfield, Milton Keynes, MK11 3LW, UK
UKHW041938210426
5322IPUK00016B/242